my **revisi⏻n** notes

AQA AS/A-level Year 1
BUSINESS

Neil James

HODDER
EDUCATION
AN HACHETTE UK COMPANY

Hachette UK's policy is to use papers that are natural, renewable and recyclable products and made from wood grown in sustainable forests. The logging and manufacturing processes are expected to conform to the environmental regulations of the country of origin.

Orders: please contact Bookpoint Ltd, 130 Milton Park, Abingdon, Oxon OX14 4SB. Telephone: (44) 01235 827720. Fax: (44) 01235 400454. Email education@bookpoint.co.uk

Lines are open from 9 a.m. to 5 p.m., Monday to Saturday, with a 24-hour message answering service. You can also order through our website: www.hoddereducation.co.uk

ISBN: 978 1 4718 4195 8

© Neil James 2015

First published in 2015 by

Hodder Education,
An Hachette UK Company
Carmelite House
50 Victoria Embankment
London EC4Y 0DZ

www.hoddereducation.co.uk

Impression number   10 9 8 7 6 5 4 3 2 1

Year   2019 2018 2017 2016 2015

Cover photo reproduced by permission of alphaspirit/Fotolia

Typeset in Integra Software Services Pvt. Ltd, Pondicherry, India

Printed in Spain

A catalogue record for this title is available from the British Library.

Get the most from this book

Everyone has to decide his or her own revision strategy, but it is essential to review your work, learn it and test your understanding. These Revision Notes will help you to do that in a planned way, topic by topic. Use this book as the cornerstone of your revision and do not hesitate to write in it — personalise your notes and check your progress by ticking off each section as you revise.

Tick to track your progress

Use the revision planner on pages 4 and 5 to plan your revision, topic by topic. Tick each box when you have:

● revised and understood a topic
● tested yourself
● practised the exam questions and gone online to check your answers and complete the quick quizzes

You can also keep track of your revision by ticking off each topic heading in the book. You may find it helpful to add your own notes as you work through each topic.

Features to help you succeed

Exam tips

Expert tips are given throughout the book to help you polish your exam technique in order to maximise your chances in the exam.

Typical mistakes

The author identifies the typical mistakes candidates make and explains how you can avoid them.

Now test yourself

These short, knowledge-based questions provide the first step in testing your learning. Answers are at the back of the book.

Definitions and key words

Clear, concise definitions of essential key terms are provided where they first appear.

Key words from the specification are highlighted in bold throughout the book.

Revision activities

These activities will help you to understand each topic in an interactive way.

Exam practice

Practice exam questions are provided for each topic. Use them to consolidate your revision and practise your exam skills.

Summaries

The summaries provide a quick-check bullet list for each topic.

Online

Go online to check your answers to the exam questions and try out the extra quick quizzes at **www.hoddereducation.co.uk/myrevisionnotes**

My revision planner

REVISED   TESTED   EXAM READY

Now test yourself answers

Exam practice answers and quick quizzes at www.hoddereducation.co.uk/myrevisionnotes

Countdown to my exams

6–8 weeks to go

- Start by looking at the specification — make sure you know exactly what material you need to revise and the style of the examination. Use the revision planner on pages 4 and 5 to familiarise yourself with the topics.
- Organise your notes, making sure you have covered everything on the specification. The revision planner will help you to group your notes into topics.
- Work out a realistic revision plan that will allow you time for relaxation. Set aside days and times for all the subjects that you need to study, and stick to your timetable.
- Set yourself sensible targets. Break your revision down into focused sessions of around 40 minutes, divided by breaks. These Revision Notes organise the basic facts into short, memorable sections to make revising easier.

REVISED ☐

4–6 weeks to go

- Read through the relevant sections of this book and refer to the exam tips, summaries, typical mistakes and key terms. Tick off the topics as you feel confident about them. Highlight those topics you find difficult and look at them again in detail.
- Test your understanding of each topic by working through the 'Now test yourself' questions and 'Revision activities' in the book. Look up the answers at the back of the book.
- Make a note of any problem areas as you revise, and ask your teacher to go over these in class.
- Look at past papers. They are one of the best ways to revise and practise your exam skills. Write or prepare planned answers to the exam practice questions provided in this book. Check your answers online and try out the extra quick quizzes at **www.hoddereducation.co.uk/ myrevisionnotes**
- Use the revision activities to try different revision methods. For example, you can make notes using mind maps, spider diagrams or flash cards.
- Track your progress using the revision planner and give yourself a reward when you have achieved your target.

REVISED ☐

One week to go

- Try to fit in at least one more timed practice of an entire past paper and seek feedback from your teacher, comparing your work closely with the mark scheme.
- Check the revision planner to make sure you haven't missed out any topics. Brush up on any areas of difficulty by talking them over with a friend or getting help from your teacher.
- Attend any revision classes put on by your teacher. Remember, he or she is an expert at preparing people for examinations.

REVISED ☐

The day before the examination

- Flick through these Revision Notes for useful reminders, for example the exam tips, summaries, typical mistakes and key terms.
- Check the time and place of your examination.
- Make sure you have everything you need — extra pens and pencils, tissues, a watch, bottled water, sweets.
- Allow some time to relax and have an early night to ensure you are fresh and alert for the examination.

REVISED ☐

My exams

Paper 1: Business 1

Date:...

Time:...

Location:...

Paper 2: Business 2

Date:...

Time:...

Location:...

1 What is business?

Understanding the nature and purpose of business

Why businesses exist

Businesses exist in many shapes and sizes and for different purposes. The opportunity for making **profit** is an important reason why they exist, but it is not the only reason. Other reasons are:

● to provide goods and services; this includes public services, such as the NHS and police and fire services
● to develop a good idea (enterprise)
● to provide help and support for others, most notably charities that raise funds in various ways to help and support the lives of others

Mission statements

A business **mission statement**, sometimes called a 'vision statement', defines what an organisation is, why it exists and its reason for being. It is a declaration of its core purpose and focus. Here are two examples:

> To passionately create innovation for our stakeholders at the intersection of chemistry, biology and physics. (**The Dow Chemical Company**)

> Bring inspiration and innovation to every athlete in the world. (**NIKE, Inc**)

The purpose of the mission statement is to help bring focus and meaning to a business and act as a guide when making critical decisions that may affect the direction of a business.

> A **mission statement** is a declaration of a business's core purpose and focus.

Common business objectives

When looking at the **objectives** of a business, it is important to remember that they are quite complex and will vary according to circumstances and the type of organisation. A charity will have different objectives to a public limited company, but even different public limited companies may have different objectives. Three key objectives of business are:

● survival
● growth
● profit

> An **objective** is a goal to help a business achieve its mission.

Over recent years the global nature of business and the intense competition in many markets has meant that two other objectives have become increasingly important, namely:

● customer service
● corporate social responsibility (CSR)

CSR refers to the commitment of business to behave ethically towards their workforce, the local community and society at large, i.e. companies take responsibility for their impact on society.

When looking at business objectives it is also important to recognise that each functional area of a business will set objectives that should contribute to the business achieving its overall objectives. This is illustrated in Figure 1.1.

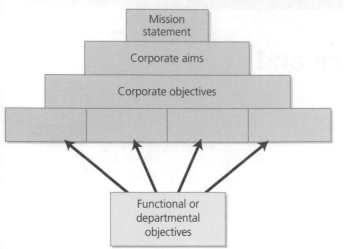

Figure 1.1 The hierarchy of objectives

Typical mistake

Do not assume that all businesses have the one objective of making a profit, or that the objectives will always be the same for a particular business. They are likely to change over time.

The relationship between mission and objectives

REVISED

The mission statement of a business outlines the bigger picture and generally establishes the core values and principles that help guide the conduct and action of staff. **Objectives**, however, are goals that are set to achieve the overall mission of the business. They differ from the mission in that they are **actionable** and **measurable**. Without the mission statement, the objectives have no direction, but without the objectives, the mission is unachievable. Putting together the mission and objectives provides a balance that helps to shape a business's operation and service.

In addition to being actionable and measurable, objectives should have the following **SMART** characteristics. They should be:
● **S**pecific: objectives must be clear, precise and well defined.
● **M**easurable: it must be possible to know when an objective has been completed.
● **A**chievable: objectives must be within capabilities and have sufficient resources.
● **R**ealistic: an objective must be challenging but possible to achieve given the capabilities and resources.
● **T**ime based: there must be a deadline to work to.

As an example, an objective for a new coffee chain entering the UK market might be increasing market share by 2.5% a year for the next 5 years. This is a SMART objective as there is a clearly defined and measurable goal, whereas simply aiming to achieve growth in market share is not.

The relative importance of different objectives is likely to vary over time depending on circumstances. In difficult economic times, survival is likely to be more important than profit or environmental targets, whereas in a booming economy, profit, growth and social issues will take on a far more important role.

Exam practice answers and quick quizzes at **www.hoddereducation.co.uk/myrevisionnotes**

Why businesses set objectives

There are a number of reasons businesses set objectives:
- The fact that objectives set will be measurable and time based means that they can be used to evaluate performance.
- If they are realistic and achievable they can provide motivation for those who are responsible. However, they should not be too easily achievable and there should be an element of challenge.
- Objectives should also be specific and, as a result, will give meaning to planning and ensure that a business remains focused on its mission.

> **Exam tip**
>
> Objectives will not be the same for all companies and will change over time. Read any stimulus material you are given in the exam carefully to ascertain which objectives are important and why for the business in question.

The measurement and importance of profit

Profit is the reward that owners or shareholders of a business receive for taking the risk of investing in the business. Profit therefore provides an incentive for setting up in business. When measuring the level of profit achieved it is first necessary to understand what is meant by revenue and the various costs involved.

Revenue is the money received from sales and is calculated by multiplying the units sold by the price of each unit. When considering revenue, be aware that other terms might be used such as **turnover**, **sales turnover** and **sales revenue** — they all mean the same thing.

Variable costs are the costs that are directly related to output and, as a result, vary directly with output. Examples include direct labour (workers who are directly involved in the production process) and raw materials.

Fixed costs, as the name suggests, are costs that are fixed and will not change in the short term. These costs will have to be paid whether or not any production takes place, and include rent, rates and director salaries.

Total costs are the fixed costs and variable costs added together and represent the total costs of production in a given time period.

Armed with figures for revenue and costs it is possible to calculate profit for a business using the formula:

profit = total revenue – total cost

> **Profit** is the amount of money remaining once all costs have been deducted from the revenue.

> **Revenue** is money received from sales.

> **Variable costs** are costs that vary as a direct result of changes in the level of output.
>
> **Fixed costs** are costs that do not change as a result of changes in the level of output.

> **Typical mistake**
>
> Make sure your definitions are complete and your examples are accurate. When defining variable costs it is not enough to say that they vary with output — they vary *directly* with output. In the same way, it is not labour that is the variable cost but labour *directly* involved with output.

> **Example**
>
> A business produces 10,000 units which it sells for £5 each. Its variable costs are £25,000 and its fixed costs £10,000.
>
> Profit = total revenue – total costs
>
> Total revenue = 10,000 × £5 = £50,000
>
> Total cost = variable costs + fixed costs = £25,000 + £10,000 = £35,000
>
> Profit = £50,000 – £35,000 = £15,000

TESTED

Now test yourself

1 List three reasons why businesses exist.
2 Outline how a mission statement differs from objectives.
3 List five business objectives.
4 Draw up a table to illustrate the likely objectives of the following: a public limited company; a public sector organisation; a charity.
5 Explain briefly why a business would write a mission statement.
6 Outline why it is necessary for any business objective to be SMART.
7 From the figures below, calculate the expected profit of ABC Ltd.
   Output: 10,000 units
   Price: £5 per unit
   Fixed costs: £5,000
   Variable costs: £3 per unit

Answers on p. 114

Understanding different business forms

Different forms of business

REVISED

Private sector businesses

Businesses in the **private sector** fall into two broad categories: corporate and non-corporate, as shown in Table 1.1.

Table 1.1 Types of business

Corporate businesses	Non-corporate businesses
Private limited companies	Sole traders (or sole proprietors)
Public limited companies	Partnerships

The **private sector** is part of the economy made up of private enterprises — businesses that are owned and controlled by individuals or groups of individuals.

Corporate businesses

Corporate businesses have a legal identity that is separate from that of their owners. Their owners benefit from limited liability. **Limited liability** restricts the financial responsibility of shareholders for a company's debts to the amount they have individually invested. It means that a company can sue and be sued and can enter into contracts. Limited liability has an important implication for the owners (shareholders) of corporate businesses because, in the event of such a business failing, the shareholders' private possessions are safe. Their liability is limited to the amount they have invested.

There are two methods by which the liability of shareholders can be limited:

- **By shares.** In this case, a shareholder's liability is limited to the value of the shares that he or she has purchased. There can be no further call on the shareholder's wealth.
- **By guarantee.** Each member's liability is restricted to the amount he/she has agreed to pay in the event of the business being wound up. This is more common with not-for-profit businesses.

Corporate businesses are businesses which have a legal identity that is separate from that of their owners.

Limited liability restricts the financial responsibility of shareholders for a company's debts to the amount they have individually invested.

There are two main types of corporate company:

- **Private limited companies.** These are normally much smaller than public limited companies. Share capital must not exceed £50,000 and 'Ltd' must be included after the company's name. The shares of a private limited company cannot be bought and sold without the agreement of other shareholders. The company's shares cannot be sold on the Stock Exchange. Private limited companies are normally relatively small and are often family businesses.
- **Public limited companies.** Their shares can be traded on the Stock Exchange and bought by any business or individual. Public limited companies must have the term 'plc' after their name. They must have a minimum capital of £50,000 by law; in practice, this figure is likely to be far higher. Public limited companies have to publish more details of their financial affairs than do private limited companies.

Those forming a company must send two main documents to the Registrar of Companies:

- **Memorandum of Association.** This sets out details of the company's name and address and its objectives in trading.
- **Articles of Association.** This details the internal arrangements of the company, including frequency of shareholders' meetings.

Once these documents have been approved, the company receives a Certificate of Incorporation and can commence trading.

Non-corporate businesses

Non-corporate businesses and their owners are not treated as separate elements — an owner's private possessions are all at risk in the event of failure. Sole traders and partners are usually said to have unlimited liability. However, since 2000 it has been possible to establish limited liability partnerships (LLPs) which offer partners financial protection.

The different types of non-corporate business are:

- **Sole traders (or proprietors).** These are businesses owned by a single person, although the business may have a number of employees. Such one-person businesses are common in retailing and services, e.g. plumbing and hairdressing.
- **Partnerships.** These comprise between two and 20 people who contribute capital and expertise to a business. A partnership is usually based on a Deed of Partnership, which states how much capital each partner has contributed, the share of profits each shall receive and the rules for electing new partners. Some partners may be 'sleeping partners', contributing capital but taking no active part in the business. Partnerships are common in the professions, e.g. dentists and accountants.

The advantages and disadvantages of the various legal forms of business are shown in Table 1.2.

Not-for-profit businesses

Not all businesses aim to make profits. A **not-for-profit business** is any organisation, such as a charity, that has business objectives other than making a profit. These businesses are also called 'social enterprises'.

Social enterprises trade in a wide range of industries and operate with a number of non-profit objectives:

- **To provide services to local communities.** Some social enterprises may remove graffiti or clean up beaches for the benefit of entire communities.

> **Typical mistake**
>
> Do not propose starting a new business as a public limited company in response to an examination question. The huge costs involved mean that this is most unlikely to happen.

> **Typical mistake**
>
> Many students argue that it is expensive and complicated to set up a private limited company. This is not true and these are not valid reasons to argue against the use of this legal form of business.

> A **not-for-profit business** is an organisation that has business objectives other than making a profit.

- **To give people job-related skills.** The television chef, Jamie Oliver, runs a chain of restaurants (called 'Fifteen') with the prime objective of providing training in a variety of catering skills for young people from disadvantaged backgrounds.
- **Fair-trading activities.** Some businesses import products from less developed countries but pay above the market price for the products. They may also invest in facilities, such as education and healthcare, in the exporting communities.

Mutuals

Mutuals are generally private businesses whose ownership base is made up of their clients and policy holders. They are characterised by the fact they are run for the benefit of their members, e.g. cooperatives. Insurance companies and building societies were traditionally organised in this way, but many of the biggest have changed to become public limited companies.

Table 1.2 The advantages and disadvantages of different legal forms of business

Type of business	Advantages	Disadvantages
Sole trader	• Simple and cheap to establish with few legal formalities. • The owner receives all the profits (if there are any). • Able to respond quickly to changes in the market. • Confidentiality is maintained as financial details do not have to be published.	• The owner is likely to be short of capital for investment and expansion. • Few assets for collateral to support applications for loans. • Unlimited liability. • It can be difficult for sole traders to take holidays.
Partnership	• Between them, partners may have a wide range of skills and knowledge. • Partners are able to raise greater amounts of capital than sole traders. • The pressure on owners is reduced as cover is available for holidays and there is support in making decisions.	• Control is shared between the partners. • Arguments are common among partners. • There is still an absolute shortage of capital — even 20 people can only raise so much. • Unlimited liability.
Private limited company	• Shareholders benefit from limited liability. • Companies have access to greater amounts of capital. • Private limited companies are only required to divulge a limited amount of financial information. • Companies have a separate legal identity.	• Private limited companies cannot sell their shares on the Stock Exchange. • Requiring permission to sell shares limits potential for flexibility and growth. • Private limited companies have to conform to a number of expensive administrative formalities.
Public limited company	• Public limited companies can gain positive publicity as a result of trading on the Stock Exchange. • Stock Exchange quotation offers access to large amounts of capital. • Stock Exchange rules are strict and this encourages investors to part with their money. • Suppliers will be more willing to offer credit to public limited companies.	• A Stock Exchange listing means emphasis is placed on short-term financial results, not long-term performance. • Public limited companies are required to publish a great deal of financial information. • Trading as a public limited company can result in significant administrative expenses.

Public sector organisations

Some services and business in the UK are controlled and run by the government or local authorities and are referred to as being in the **public sector**. This includes services such as police, fire, the BBC and the NHS as well as local council run services such as rubbish collection. This sector used to include a number of key industries and utilities such as coal, steel, water, telephone etc. that were known as 'nationalised industries'. These have largely been sold off to the private sector through a **privatisation** process.

The **public sector** is part of the economy that is owned and controlled by the government or local authorities.

Privatisation is the process of converting government owned and controlled industries/businesses to the private sector.

Now test yourself

TESTED

8 Identify three differences between a corporate business and a non-corporate business.
9 Using examples, define the public sector.
10 List and explain three objectives that a not-for-profit business may have.
11 How does a mutual organisation differ from other incorporated business organisations?

Answers on p. 114

Reasons for choosing different forms of business

REVISED

The key choice in terms of business structure is between **unincorporated** and **incorporated** status. There are a number of factors that may be considered here:

- **Formalities and expenses.** Sole traders and partnerships are relatively easy to set up with few formalities. This is an ideal form for small businesses such as joiners, electricians and corner shops.
- **Size and risk**. If a business is and intends to remain small and carries little in the way of risk, then a sole trader or partnership may be the most appropriate form of business. This is the reason many corner shops, joiners and electricians remain as sole traders.
- **Objectives of the owners**. If the objectives of the owners involve growth, then forming an incorporated business might be more appropriate. This is likely to give greater access to capital and limited liability would reduce the risks involved for the owners.

Reasons for changing business form

REVISED

The main reasons for changing business form are as follows:

- **Circumstances.** Due to changing circumstances, such as the growth of a business, the owner/s may wish to become incorporated in order to benefit from limited liability.
- **Capital.** The owner/s of a business may find it easier to raise capital by becoming incorporated or by becoming a public limited company if it is a private limited company.
- **Acquisition or takeover.** This may cause a change of structure, e.g. a private limited company may be taken over by a public limited company.

Although businesses generally change from private limited to public limited, it is also possible to move the other way, i.e. from public to private limited. A business may do this to escape the constant scrutiny of the city and the pressure of short-term shareholder objectives. A good example of this is Richard Branson's Virgin.

The role of shareholders and why they invest

REVISED

Ordinary share capital is the money invested in a company by **shareholders** entitling them to part ownership of the company. This capital is permanent and will never have to be paid back to the owners by the company. If the owners wish to get their money back, they can sell their shares through the stock market. Private individuals can invest in public limited companies, becoming shareholders and part-owners of the business, but private individuals will only ever own a small fraction of the shares of any one business. By far the biggest shareholders will be financial institutions such as pension funds and insurance companies.

Shareholders have certain rights and a role to play in the running of a business. Major decisions that will have an impact on shareholders are required to be approved by the shareholders at a general meeting called by the directors. The main role of shareholders therefore is to attend this meeting and discuss whatever is on the agenda and to ensure the directors do not go beyond their powers. There are also only certain actions that can be done by shareholders, such as the removal of directors or changing the name of a company.

There are two reasons why private individuals and financial institutions invest in shares:
● **Income.** Shareholders are entitled to a share of company profits known as a 'dividend'. The total amount given to shareholders is decided by the board of directors and can vary, but investors hope that the return they get will increase over time.
● **Capital growth.** Shareholders hope that the value of their shares will increase over time.

Influences on and the significance of share price changes

REVISED

Both the level of dividend and the share price of a company can fluctuate, and it is important to recognise that they can go down in value as well as up. The price of an individual share is determined through the market. If demand is greater than supply the price will go up; if there are more sellers than buyers the price will fall. There are a number of reasons why shares and dividend may fluctuate in value:
● **Performance.** If there are worse than expected profits, e.g. if a retailer reports a poor performance during the Christmas period, a time when traditionally sales are good, shares will go down in value. If profits are higher, then share values will increase.

- **Expectation of better or worse profit performance.** This might be as a result of a new product due to be launched on the market.
- **Changes within the market or competitive environment.** For example, the move of consumers from the mainstream supermarkets such as Tesco to the discounters such as Lidl and Aldi will adversely affect the value of Tesco's shares.
- **World uncertainty.** Conflict in the Middle East, for example, or an economic downturn will cause share prices to fluctuate.

Market capitalisation is calculated by taking the share price and multiplying it by the number of shares issued. This gives a valuation of a company. Changes in the share price will therefore affect the valuation of a business. A falling share price might provide an opportunity for investment or even takeover, or it might be an indication of a business in decline.

Exam tip

An economic downturn may be bad for some businesses, but for others it may be good (Tesco v. Aldi). The same can be said about conflict in the Middle East — this is bad for some businesses, but arms manufacturers are likely to benefit.

Market capitalisation is calculated as follows:

share price × number of shares issued

The effects of ownership on mission, objectives, decisions and performance

Profit is a key objective of many private sector businesses, and for some this may dominate the decision-making process.

Public limited companies are owned by shareholders who are often driven by profit, which can lead to a short-term approach to business. Decision-making will be made on the basis of achieving profit, and the philosophy outlined in the mission statement may take a back seat. This emphasis on profit has been demonstrated by Tesco. In 2014, Tesco saw falling profits and made mistakes in reporting profits higher than they actually were. These failings led to a big fall in its share price and the resignation of its CEO.

Sole traders and private limited companies, however, will be less affected by this need to achieve profits, and may be able to keep a closer focus on their mission statement and objectives.

Now test yourself

14 Briefly give two reasons why people invest in shares.
15 List four reasons why share prices may fluctuate.
16 XYZ plc has a share price of 57p and 2,100 million shares. What is its market capitalisation?

Answers on p. 114

Understanding that businesses operate within an external environment

The world businesses operate in is both unpredictable and uncertain, and changes in this external environment will have an impact on the demand for goods and services, costs and the way a business operates generally.

How the external environment can affect costs and demand

The external environment refers to aspects that are out of the control of the business and include competition, market conditions, economic factors (such as incomes and interest rates), social and environmental issues and demographic factors. These factors not only affect demand for a product or service and the costs of operating a business, but also impact on its ability to achieve its strategic goals and objectives. Some of these influences may be predictable in that trends can be spotted in a particular market, but others, such as the recession of 2008, are less predictable. Whether predictable or not, a business is likely to have to take action to prepare for or respond to the changing circumstances.

Exam tip

Do not always assume that any change in the external environment will be negative. Sometimes changes can be positive for a business, and what is negative for one might be positive for another.

Competition

Almost all businesses operate within a competitive environment, competing against other businesses that offer the same or similar goods. The strategies adopted by competitor firms will therefore have an impact on a business. For example, we have seen the impact of competition on the grocery industry with the big four of Tesco, Asda, Sainsburys and Morrisons all suffering lower demand as a result of the discount retailers Aldi and Lidl. It is important, therefore, that a business tries to differentiate its own products or services in order to encourage consumers to purchase its products or services.

Furthermore, sometimes a competitor will come up with an innovative product or service, such as Apple with the iPod and iPhone, which have had huge impact on the markets they operate in. Some businesses have also been quicker to use technology in their operations and have benefited, whereas others, such as Morrisons, were slow to adopt internet selling and suffered as a result. HMV did not anticipate the rise in downloading of music, films and books and almost went out of business.

Not only can competition have an impact on demand, but it can also have an impact on costs. In a competitive environment, firms are likely to compete on price, and this is likely to lead to pressure on costs with individual firms looking to reduce costs wherever possible.

Market conditions

Market conditions refer to the characteristics of a particular market and might include its size, growth rate, any barriers to entry, seasonal factors and the amount and intensity of competition. All these factors will have an impact on a business in terms of demand and costs. For instance, a market with high market growth and a low intensity of competitiveness is likely to present greater opportunities for higher demand than the opposite. A market with high barriers to entry, such as the aeronautical engine market, will protect operators in this market from new entrants.

Economic factors

Economic factors include the stage of the economic cycle, interest rates, inflation, and exchange rates. It is, however, interest rates and incomes that are the focus of the AS specification.

Interest rates

Changes in interest rates can have a big impact on both the demand for goods and services provided by a business and its cost. This impact may be positive for some businesses but negative for others. Rising interest rates generally result in lower demand, as consumers are likely to have less disposable income due to higher borrowing costs for loans and mortgages. Other consumers might also be encouraged to save more as a result of rising interest rates. Not all businesses will be affected negatively though — discount retailers might actually benefit as consumers switch from traditional grocery stores such as Tesco to ones such as Lidl. It has also been shown that restaurants, such as Pizza Hut, have gained as consumers have cut back on spending.

Costs will also be affected by changes in interest rates. A business with high levels of borrowing will be faced by higher costs when interest rates rise. This, coupled with any fall in demand, can be crippling for some businesses. Again, not all businesses will be affected in the same way — those with little in the way of borrowing will be less affected by interest rate rises. Should interest rates fall it is likely to have the opposite effect on both demand and costs.

Interest rates can also affect a business in terms of decision-making: high or rising interest rates may lead to a business postponing new capital investment due to the costs involved. Low or falling interest rates will be more conducive to capital investment. Finally, if a business has large cash reserves, it could benefit from rising interest rates due to the higher interest received.

Incomes

Demand in the economy will also be affected by the level of incomes. Falling incomes, as in the recession of 2008, saw falling demand, whereas as the economy has picked up and income has risen, demand has increased. It should, however be recognised that not all businesses will be affected to the same extent — demand for necessities will be less affected by changes in income than demand for luxuries. This is discussed in more detail in the section on income elasticity on pp. 38–39.

Demographic factors

Demography is the study of human populations and includes factors such as the age, gender, income and occupation of the population as well as the birth and death rates, the level of public health and immigration. In the UK, not only is the population growing with immigration making a large contribution to this growth, it is also an ageing population. These factors affect the level of demand and the nature of the goods and services purchased. They also affect the structure of the working population itself. As a result, workers are now facing the prospect of working longer before they receive the state pension. Some businesses, such as B&Q, actively seek to recruit older workers, and the demand for holidays such as cruises has increased over recent years. It is therefore important for businesses to recognise and anticipate the demographic changes taking place.

Environmental issues and fair trade

Businesses ignore environmental issues today at their peril. The influence of the media and social media means that any misdemeanour in terms of pollution and exploitation of people in less developed countries is quickly brought to light. This can then have an impact on reputation, the sales and the costs of a business.

In the UK, successive governments have introduced legislation to help protect the environment from pollution. As a result, businesses have to spend large amounts on measures to ensure that water, air and the surrounding countryside are kept free of pollution. Some businesses have

> **Exam tip**
>
> When looking at interest rates and income, be aware of the interrelationship between them. A rise in interest rates will indirectly cause a fall in the income available to consumers to spend (disposable income), whereas a fall will have the opposite effect.

located themselves overseas where legislation is less stringent, but even there they are not always free from the public gaze.

Concern for the environment is being driven by factors such as global warming. It is believed that carbon emissions are the major contributing factor to global warming and that not just businesses but governments should be doing more to cut these emissions. Sustainable development has also become an issue due to the worry that certain resources are running out and that we should try and conserve and sustain them wherever possible, e.g. the fishing industry is subject to quotas and some paper manufacturers now say they plant one new tree for every one cut down.

Fair trade has also become a concern. This is about achieving better prices, decent working conditions and fair terms of trade for farmers and workers in less developed countries. This is likely to mean higher costs for a business, but could also lead to greater demand, better reputation and could act as a selling point.

These external factors (see Figure 1.2) can have a significant impact on the demand for products and services provided, the costs incurred and profit. Although a business might sometimes be caught out by sudden changes in the external environment (e.g. the recession of 2008 and its depth), it should be able to anticipate and plan for some changes. For instance, demographic changes can be identified, changes in interest rates anticipated and new products and services provided in order to stay ahead of competitors. As a result, any negative impact on cost and demand may be minimised and any positive impact maximised.

> **Exam tip**
>
> The external factors affecting a business can be easily recalled using the acronym PESTLE: **P**olitical, **E**conomic, **S**ocial, **T**echnological, **L**egal and **E**nvironmental.

POLITICS	• Government type and policy • Funding, grants and initiatives
ECONOMY	• Inflation and interest rates • Labour and energy costs
SOCIAL	• Population, education, media • Lifestyle, fashion, culture
TECHNOLOGY	• Emerging technologies, web • Information and communication
LEGAL	• Regulations and standards • Employment law
ENVIRONMENT	• Weather, green and ethical issues • Pollution, waste, recycling

Figure 1.2 External factors affecting businesses

Now test yourself

TESTED

17 Briefly explain why it is important for a business to differentiate its product or service in a competitive market.
18 How might a manufacturer of luxury products be affected by a rise in interest rates?
19 List three reasons why a study of demographics might be important to a business.
20 What do you understand by the term 'fair trade'?

Answers on pp. 114–115

Exam practice

XYZ plc

When XYZ plc converted to a public limited company, everything seemed rosy. It had a mission of being the best in the business and objectives of both market growth and growth of market share. Three years on and things seemed very different: customer complaints had increased and the company had failed to hit its targets for market growth and share. Understandably, shareholders were very unhappy with the steadily declining share price and lack of dividends. Although its problems had for the most part been caused by the changing external environment with rising interest rates and an increasingly competitive market, it was also clear XYZ plc was inadequately prepared for the change to public status.

Key data of XYZ plc

	At flotation	Present
Sales	£25m	£27.5m
Market share	5.3%	5.2%
Share price	50p	35p
Number of shares	100m	100m

Questions

a Calculate the change in market capitalisation of XYZ plc.   [4]
b Explain why although sales have increased, XYZ plc market share has decreased.   [6]
c Analyse the factors shareholders may have considered before investing in XYZ plc.   [9]
d To what extent do you believe XYZ plc was correct in its decision to convert to a public limited company?   [16]

Answers and quick quiz 1 online

ONLINE

Summary

You should now have an understanding of all the points below.

Understanding the nature and purpose of business

- why businesses exist
- common business objectives and their purpose
- the relationship between mission and objectives
- the measurement and importance of profit covering revenue, fixed costs, variable costs and total costs

Understanding the different forms of business

- the reasons for choosing different forms of business and for changing business form including sole traders, private and public limited companies, non-profit organisations as well as public sector organisations
- limited and unlimited liability
- ordinary share capital, market capitalisation and dividends
- the role of shareholders and why they invest
- influences on share price and the significance of share price changes
- the effects of ownership on mission, objectives, decisions and performance

Understanding that businesses operate within an external environment

- how the following external factors affect costs and demand: competition, market conditions, incomes, interest rates, demographic factors, environmental issues and fair trade

2 Managers, leadership and decision-making

Understanding management, leadership and decision-making

What managers do

Peter Drucker, who some look upon as the creator of the modern study of management, outlined five basic tasks of a manager:

1 **Set objectives.** The manager sets goals for a group and decides what work needs to be done.
2 **Organise.** The manager divides the work into manageable activities and selects the people to undertake them.
3 **Motivate and communicate.** The manager creates a team that works together.
4 **Measure.** The manager not only sets targets but analyses and appraises performance.
5 **Develop people.** It is up to the manager to develop people, who may be looked upon as the most important asset of a business.

Henri Fayol also outlined five elements of management: planning, organising, commanding, coordinating and controlling.

The role of a manager then is varied, but can be summed up in four key tasks: they **plan**, **organise**, **direct** and **control**.

Types of management and leadership styles

Leadership style is the way in which a leader approaches his/her role of planning, organising, directing and controlling. There are three basic styles of leadership:

- **Autocratic leaders**, who make decisions without consulting others.
- **Democratic leaders**, who make the final decision but include others in the process.
- **Laissez-faire leaders**, who allow team members freedom if they do their work and meet deadlines.

Other styles of leadership include **charismatic leaders**, who believe they can do no wrong, **paternalistic leaders**, who consult and try to make decisions in the best interest of all, and **bureaucratic leaders**, who do everything exactly by the rules.

This range of leadership styles is illustrated by the Tannenbaum Schmidt continuum (see Figure 2.1). This classifies the style according to how much a leader tells or listens to his/her staff.

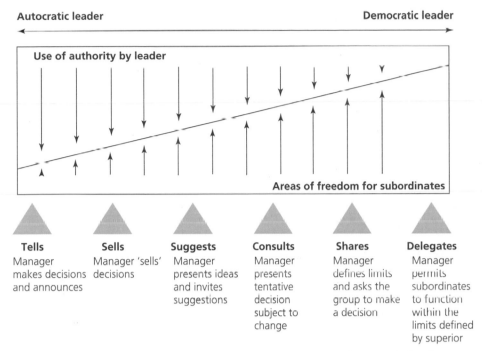

Tells
Manager makes decisions and announces

Sells
Manager 'sells' decisions

Suggests
Manager presents ideas and invites suggestions

Consults
Manager presents tentative decision subject to change

Shares
Manager defines limits and asks the group to make a decision

Delegates
Manager permits subordinates to function within the limits defined by superior

Figure 2.1 Tannenbaum and Schmidt's continuum of leadership behaviour

The figure shows the relationship between the level of freedom in decision-making a manager gives to a team of workers and the level of authority retained by the manager. As the workers' freedom increases, so the manager's authority decreases.

A further study of leadership by Blake and Mouton portrays leadership through a grid depicting concern for people on the y axis and concern for production on the x axis with each dimension ranging from 1 to 9. This results in five leadership styles as shown in Figure 2.2 and outlined below.

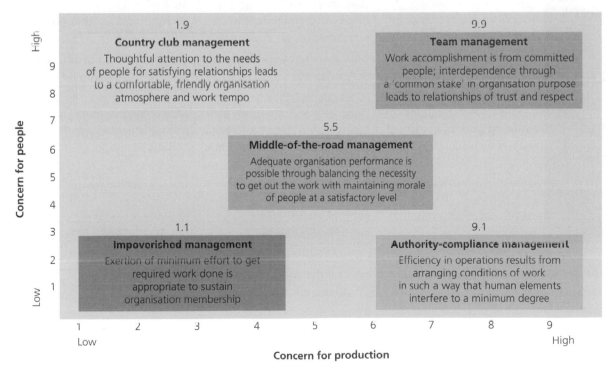

Figure 2.2 Blake and Mouton's leadership grid

- **Country club management.** The emphasis is on people, with little concern for the task. This style may hamper production as it relies on workers being motivated.

- **Authority–compliance management.** Leadership here is autocratic with a clear emphasis on the task and little concern for people. It may increase production, but employees are likely to be unhappy.
- **Impoverished management (produce or perish).** Leadership will be ineffective with little concern for either the task or the people.
- **Middle-of-the-road management.** There is a compromise here with some focus on people and some on the task, but it is likely to lead to average performance.
- **Team management.** This style focuses on both the task and the people. It is likely to be the most effective, with emphasis on empowerment, trust and team working.

The effectiveness of different styles of leadership and management and influences on these

REVISED

The effectiveness of different styles of leadership is summarised in Table 2.1.

Table 2.1 Leadership styles

	Democratic	Authoritarian	Laissez-faire
Description	Democratic leadership entails running a business on the basis of decisions agreed by the majority.	An authoritarian leadership style keeps information and decision-making among the senior managers.	Laissez-faire leadership means the leader has a peripheral role, leaving staff to manage the business.
Key features	Encourages participation and makes use of delegation.	Sets objectives and allocates tasks. Leader retains control throughout.	Leader evades duties of management and uncoordinated delegation occurs.
Communication	Extensive, two-way. Encourages contributions from subordinates.	One-way communications downwards from leader to subordinates.	Mainly horizontal communication, though little communication occurs.
Uses	When complex decisions are made requiring a range of specialist skills.	Useful when quick decisions are required.	Can encourage production of highly creative work by subordinates.
Advantages	Commitment to business, satisfaction and quality of work may all improve.	Decisions and direction of business will be consistent. May project image of confident, well-managed business.	May bring the best out of highly professional or creative groups.
Disadvantages	Slow decision-making and need for consensus may avoid taking 'best' decisions.	Lack of information, so subordinates are highly dependent on leaders; supervision needed.	May not be deliberate, but bad management — staff lack of focus and sense of direction. Much dissatisfaction.

Different leaders adopt different styles of leadership and the style adopted will vary according to the individual and the circumstances involved. Key influences might be:

- **The individual.** Some leaders feel they always have to be in control and may lean more towards an autocratic approach, whereas others may feel more comfortable discussing decisions and will be more democratic in their approach. In other words, the style adopted will depend on the leader's personality and skills.
- **Nature of the industry.** Some industries require a high degree of creativity, whereas with others safety might be paramount.

Typical mistake

Do not assume that a democratic style of leadership is always the best style to adopt — it will depend on the circumstances of the individual business.

Exam practice answers and quick quizzes at **www.hoddereducation.co.uk/myrevisionnotes**

The leadership style adopted is likely to reflect this with a more laissez-faire approach adopted where creativity is needed and a more autocratic approach where safety is of concern.

- **Business culture.** If a business has a tradition of doing things in a particular way, then this might determine the style adopted. It may have always operated with a more laissez-faire or autocratic approach that might prove difficult to change.

> **Exam tip**
>
> Do not assume that there is one best style of leadership, as the style adopted is likely to depend on and evolve with the circumstances a business finds itself in.

TESTED

Now test yourself

1 Identify four key aspects of a leader's role.
2 State three influences on leadership style.
3 Identify one key feature of a democratic leader and one key feature of a laissez-faire leader.
4 How are leaders classified in the Tannenbaum Schmidt continuum?

Answers on p. 115

Understanding management decision-making

The value of decision-making based on data (scientific decision-making) and on intuition

REVISED

Scientific decision-making is the systematic approach of collecting facts and applying logical decision-making techniques, such as decision trees, to the decision-making process. The alternative to this approach is trial and error and intuition (gut feeling).

> **Scientific decision-making** is decision-making based on data that uses a logical and rational approach.

In business there are uncertainties involved with any decision. These may stem from the market, the economy, the consumer, competitors and even how the various functional areas within a business will react to a decision. When making decisions, managers do so in the expectation that there will be some reward in terms of achieving objectives. Any decision made, however, will involve some risk, and it is for this reason that a scientific approach to decision-making may be adopted — to reduce risk. This involves the collection and analysis of data and the use of analytical tools in the forming of decisions. Examples of analytical tools include the Boston matrix, product life cycle, investment appraisal and ratio analysis as well as decision trees, which are investigated below.

Opportunity cost

Managers may also consider the **opportunity cost** when making a decision. This is the cost of the next best alternative that will be missed by making a particular decision. Business resources, particularly finance, are limited and, as a result, a business will not be able to undertake everything it would like: it will have to make a choice. For example, by investing in a new fleet of vehicles it may miss out on a new computer system — the computer system represents the opportunity cost.

> **Opportunity cost** — the next best alternative forgone.

Intuition

Intuition refers to decisions that are made on a gut feeling rather than based on evidence and rational processes. Data are not always correct. For example, the decision by Coca-Cola to change its recipe in response

> **Intuition** is making decisions based on gut feeling rather than data and rational analysis.

to taste tests proved to be a marketing disaster. For other innovative products it may be impossible to judge consumer reaction if they have never seen the product. If an analytical approach had been adopted, the Sony Walkman and probably the MP3 player would never have been introduced to the market. Intuition then will always be an important factor in decision-making.

The use and value of decision trees in decision-making

Decision trees are tree-like diagrams that can be used to determine the optimum course of action in situations where several possible alternatives with uncertain outcomes exist. They are a visual representation of the various risks, rewards and potential value of each option.

> **Decision trees** are tree-like diagrams showing various options, their probabilities and financial outcomes.

Drawing and evaluating a decision tree

Every decision tree begins with a square. This represents the decision to be made:

At least two lines will come out of the square representing the possible options. There will often be a third line — the do-nothing option:

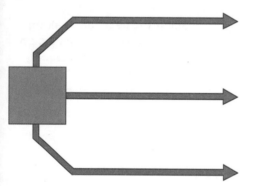

Taking each line in turn it is now necessary to decide whether it is a result, uncertain or another decision has to be made.

For a result there is no more to do, uncertain is represented by a circle and a decision by another square. The do-nothing line is a result and for our purposes we will assume there are no further decisions (note more complicated decision trees are likely to have further decisions). The resulting decision tree will be as follows:

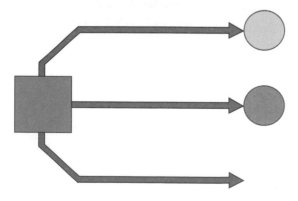

Exam practice answers and quick quizzes at **www.hoddereducation.co.uk/myrevisionnotes**

From each circle, lines will be drawn showing the possible outcomes:

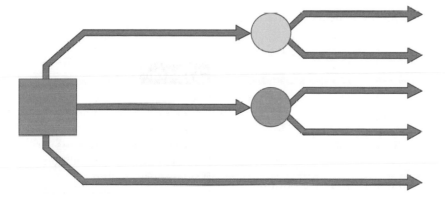

In order to evaluate the decision tree, all lines need to be fully labelled. This means indicating the following information on the decision tree:
● the cost of each option
● the potential outcomes
● the probabilities

This is shown in Figure 2.3. XYZ plc is considering whether to relaunch an existing product that has been failing or whether to undertake the development and launch of a completely new product. The data in Table 2.2 relates to each.

Table 2.2 XYZ plc relaunch and new product data

	Relaunch existing product	New product
Cost	£2.5m	£6m
Outcome success	£8.5m	£12m
Outcome failure	£0.5m	£2m
Probability success	0.7	0.6
Probability failure	0.3	0.4

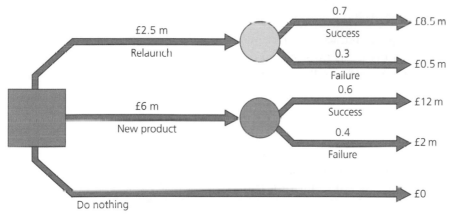

Figure 2.3 Decision tree for XYZ plc

Finally, it is necessary to calculate the expected values.

For each circle the outcomes are multiplied with the probabilities and added together. The cost of that option is then subtracted. Each option can then be compared to see which provides the highest return.

In the example above the calculation is as follows:

Relaunch

(£8.5m × 0.7 + £0.5m × 0.3) – £2.5m

£5.95 + £0.15 – £2.5m = **£3.6m**

New product

(£12m × 0.6 + £2m × 0.4) – £6m

£7.2m + £0.8m – £6m = **£2m**

From these calculations relaunch would be the most lucrative option.

Decision trees can be a useful analytical tool as they make managers think and quantify decisions rather than just go by intuition. They do, however, have limitations as managers may be influenced by their own bias towards one decision rather than another. In other words, they may make the returns for their favoured approach more attractive and thereby justify their decision. There is also the problem with establishing probabilities: it may be possible to base these on past experience, but even so they are likely to be just guesstimates.

> **Exam tip**
>
> Although the AQA specification does not require students to construct decision trees, an ability to do so will certainly aid understanding.

Now test yourself

TESTED

5 Identify three key pieces of information required for a decision tree.
6 Briefly outline the benefits and drawbacks of decision trees.

Answers on p. 115

Influences on decision-making

REVISED

There are a number of influences on decision-making as outlined below.

Mission and objectives

The mission of a business is its essential purpose and, to some extent, a business will be guided in its decision-making by its mission and the objectives it sets. For example, decision-making at Poundland will be influenced by its pricing policy.

Ethics

Ethics is about making decisions that are morally correct. The growth in fair trade products such as chocolate and coffee illustrates how some businesses have been influenced by this in their decision-making.

External environment

The external environment may have a big impact on decision-making. A downturn in the economy or rise in interest rates could see decisions being postponed or even totally abandoned, whereas an expanding economy or fall in interest rates might see decisions being brought forward. Decision-making will also be influenced by changing demographics, (e.g. the growing elderly population), increased environmental awareness and by changes in the law.

Competition

All business operates within a competitive environment and decisions will be influenced by this. Some business decision-making will be aimed at first-mover advantage and getting ahead of competition, whereas other decision-making will simply be responding to the action of competitors. The major supermarket chains, for example, have all been forced to respond to the actions of the discount retailers such as Aldi and Lidl.

Resource constraints

A business will only be able to do what it is physically possible to do. Production capacity, skills of the workforce and financial resources will, in the short term, limit what a business can do. In the long term, it may be possible to overcome these constraints, but a business needs to be certain about any decision being made.

> **Exam tip**
>
> In making a decision a business is likely to consider the opportunity cost and will be limited by the resources available.

> **Now test yourself** TESTED
>
> 7 Briefly outline how the external environment may impact on decision-making.
> 8 List four other influences on decision-making.
>
> **Answers on p. 115**

Understanding the role and importance of stakeholders

The need to consider stakeholder needs when making decisions

REVISED

The various **stakeholders** and their interests are outlined below:
- **employees:** job security, good working conditions and pay
- **customers:** good customer service and value for money
- **shareholders:** capital growth and dividends
- **suppliers:** regular orders and on-time payment
- **local communities:** avoidance of pollution and congestion, employment
- **government:** employment, payment of taxes

Decisions taken by business will have an impact on the various stakeholders so it is important to consider and manage these needs.

> A **stakeholder** is any individual or group who has an interest in the activities and performance of a business.

Stakeholder mapping

Stakeholder analysis and management is important in decision-making and to this end A. Mendelow drew up the matrix shown in Figure 2.4.

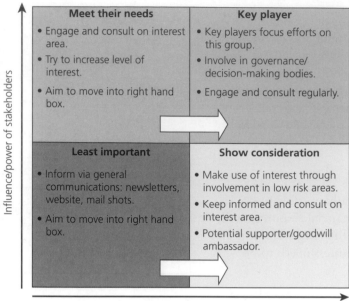

Figure 2.4 Mendelow's matrix

In this matrix (or stakeholder map), stakeholders are categorised according to the amount of power they have and their level of interest. Those with high power and high interest are key players, and management needs to keep this group happy, perhaps by involving them in the decision-making process. Those with low power and interest require minimal effort, perhaps simply keeping them up to date with what is happening. Those with high power and little interest need to be consulted and, if possible, have their level of interest increased in order to avoid potential conflicts at a later date. Those with high interest and little power need to be kept informed and up to date in order to avoid potential conflicts and enhance the reputation of the business as a considerate business.

Stakeholder needs and the possible overlap and conflict of these needs

REVISED

The potential overlap and conflict of stakeholder interests are illustrated in Table 2.3 below.

Table 2.3 Potential overlap and conflict of stakeholder interests

Decision	Overlap	Conflict
Relocate overseas	• **Shareholders:** potential for lower costs and increased profit. • **Management:** achieve objectives in terms of costs and profit.	• **Local community:** impact on local economy. • **Employees:** lost jobs. • **Government:** less tax.
Introduce new technology	• **Shareholders and management:** lower costs and potential profit. • **Consumer:** may result in better quality and reliability.	• **Employees:** may lose jobs. • **Less employment:** could impact on local community.
Expand production	• **Shareholders:** higher sales and profit. • **Employees:** job opportunities. • **Customers:** greater availability. • **Suppliers:** more orders. • **Government:** tax. • **Community:** greater production.	• **Local community:** greater congestion and pollution.

Exam practice answers and quick quizzes at **www.hoddereducation.co.uk/myrevisionnotes**

Decision	Overlap	Conflict
Increase price	• **Shareholders:** potential profit increase. • **Management:** improved performance. • **Government:** more tax.	• **Customers:** cost more.
Cut costs	• **Shareholders:** potential profit. • **Management:** achieving objectives.	• **Employees:** potential job loss. • **Customers:** quality might be affected. • **Suppliers:** pressure on prices.
Enter new markets/ products	• **Shareholders:** potential profit. • **Employees:** job security. • **Suppliers:** increased orders. • **Community:** greater employment.	• **Local community:** pollution due to increased production.

Influences on the relationship with stakeholders

REVISED

There are a number of influences on the relationship with stakeholders, one of which is the power and interest of individual stakeholders as illustrated by stakeholder mapping. Other influences include:

- **Leadership styles.** The style of leadership may have an impact: an authoritarian leader may have little concern for individual stakeholder groups and would be unlikely to consult them. A more democratic leader, however, would be more likely to consult individual stakeholders when making decisions.
- **Business objectives.** Some businesses may be committed to an ethical approach in their decision-making whilst others may be less concerned. For example, The Body Shop is committed to not testing on animals and therefore attracts less attention from pressure groups.
- **Government.** Legislation introduced by the government (or EU) can affect relationships with stakeholders. Examples include legislation regarding employment, the environment or safety.
- **State of economy.** When economic and market conditions are booming, it is easier for a business to address issues related to stakeholders. In these circumstances there is likely to be greater access to finance to improve working conditions and environmental aspects. The opposite is the case when the economy or market is in decline.

How to manage the relationship with different stakeholders

REVISED

Although there is always potential for conflict between stakeholders, this can be significantly reduced if managed correctly. Stakeholder mapping gives an indication of how this might be managed in terms of recognising those stakeholders with the greatest power and interest in a decision. Key to the management, however, is good communication, involvement and participation in any decisions being made. If there is a culture of good communication and consultation of stakeholder groups in decisions, the likelihood of conflict can be minimised. Careful planning and introduction of decisions may reduce the impact on individual groups. For instance, it might be possible to phase in new technology, which might avoid the need for redundancies.

> **Exam tip**
>
> When evaluating the conflict of interest between stakeholder groups a short-versus long-term approach is often useful.

Now test yourself

9 Draw up a table to show four stakeholder groups and their interest in a manufacturing business.
10 How does Mendelow categorise stakeholders in his matrix?
11 Besides the power and interest of individual stakeholders, identify four other influences on the relationship with stakeholders.
12 Briefly outline the key to managing stakeholder relations.

Answers on p. 115

Exam practice

McTavish's shortbread

Hamish McTavish was used to getting his own way, and as the majority shareholder in the family business, this had been easy to achieve. His latest idea, however, was rather more controversial and was likely to split the board of directors unless he could convince them otherwise. He had been very successful in developing the shortbread biscuit business and establishing a highly respected brand name within Scotland. He wanted to diversify into other biscuits and cakes, but the other directors wanted to expand the core area throughout the UK. In order to support his case, he adopted a scientific decision-making approach and drew up the decision tree below.

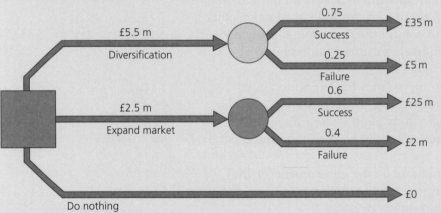

Would this be enough to convince the other directors or would Hamish just have to follow his intuition and force this through anyway?

Questions

a How does intuition differ from scientific decision-making?   [4]
b Using the decision tree above calculate the difference in outcome between expansion and diversification.   [6]
c Analyse the potential problems Hamish might face in forcing through the decision of diversification. [9]
d Evaluate the extent to which using the scientific approach to decision-making is the right approach for Hamish to take.   [16]

Answers and quick quiz 2 online

Summary

You should now have an understanding of all the points below.

Understanding management, leadership and decision-making

- the role of managers including objective setting, analysing, leading, making decisions and reviewing
- types of management and leadership styles, their effectiveness and influences on them
- theories of management including the Tannenbaum Schmidt continuum and the Blake Mouton grid

Understanding management decision-making

- the risks, rewards, uncertainty and opportunity costs involved in decision-making

- the distinction between scientific decision-making and intuition
- the use and value of decision trees, including the ability to interpret and calculate expected values and net gains
- influences on decision-making: mission, objectives, ethics, external environment and resource constraints

Understanding the role and importance of stakeholders

- the consideration of stakeholder needs in decision-making and stakeholder mapping
- the possible overlap and conflict of stakeholder needs
- influences on and management of stakeholder relations

3 Decision-making to improve marketing performance

Marketing is the business function that provides the link between the business and the consumer. The Chartered Institute of Marketing defines marketing as 'the process responsible for identifying, anticipating and satisfying customer requirements profitably'.

Setting marketing objectives

Marketing objectives should be a part of the overall corporate business objectives and sit within the overall business plan and strategy. Objectives might include:

- **Sales volume and sales value.** Sales volume is the number of units sold and sales value is how much the sales are worth, e.g. in pounds sterling.
- **Market size.** In itself this is difficult to use as an objective, but a knowledge of market size will give an indication of the potential market. This would enable realistic targets to be set for sales, growth, and share.
- **Market and sales growth.** This would involve targeting an increase in overall sales in order to either maintain market share (in a growing market) or improve it.
- **Market share.** This is the proportion of a particular market that is controlled by an individual business. Increasing **market share** is likely to bring benefits for a business, such as brand loyalty and greater revenue.
- **Brand loyalty.** Achieving sales is one thing, but what businesses want is for customers to come back time after time. In other words, businesses want to achieve **brand loyalty**.

> **Typical mistake**
>
> Students sometimes assume that just because sales may be growing, market share automatically increases. This is not always the case, as in a growing market an individual business's sales may be increasing at a slower rate than others in the market.

> **Market share** is the percentage of a market's total sales that is earned by a particular company over a specified time period.
>
> **Brand loyalty** is when consumers become committed to a particular brand and make repeat purchases over time.

The value of setting marketing objectives

REVISED

The value of setting objectives might include the following:

- **Target setting.** This gives the business a focus and sense of direction.
- **Motivation.** Objectives can be motivating for those responsible.
- **Evaluation of performance.** As with all objectives, they need to be SMART: **S**pecific, **M**easurable, **A**chievable, **R**ealistic and **T**ime based. All of the marketing objectives outlined above are quantifiable and therefore measurable. As a result, they can be used to judge performance.

Possible calculations

- **Market share:** sales of firm/total market sales × 100
- **Sales growth:** difference in sales/earliest year × 100
- **Market growth:** difference in sales/earliest year × 100
- **Market size:** (sales/market share) × 100

> **Exam tip**
>
> The calculations you will be asked to perform in examinations are normally straightforward provided you have learned the formula and practised them regularly.

External and internal influences on marketing objectives and decisions

REVISED

External influences include:

- **Market and competition.** Marketing objectives are likely to vary according to whether the market is growing or static, and depending on the actions of competitors.

Exam practice answers and quick quizzes at **www.hoddereducation.co.uk/myrevisionnotes**

- **Economic factors.** Factors such as the stage of the economic cycle and interest rates will influence objectives as they will affect consumer spending.
- **Social factors.** Over time, consumer tastes and fashion change and this needs to be reflected in marketing objectives.
- **Ethics.** Since consumers are more aware of ethical issues, many businesses have reviewed their marketing objectives to reflect this. This can be seen in the move to promote fair trade products and the fact they do not exploit workers in sweat shops.
- **Technology.** This has had a big impact on the way businesses both produce and sell their goods and services. Growth of online sales and the facility for consumers to design their own products (mass customisation) have had a major impact on marketing objectives.

Internal influences include:
- **Finance available.** All marketing functions need to operate within the budget allocated, although a business whose finances are in a healthy state will be able to allocate larger amounts to marketing.
- **Production capacity.** The marketing function must liaise with the operations function in order to ensure that is it physically possible to achieve any targets set for sales growth.
- **Human resources.** Objectives set must also take into account the size and capabilities of the workforce. Increasing market share might be difficult without further recruitment and training.
- **Nature of product.** Any objectives set need to reflect the nature of the product. Innovative products might have considerable scope for growth, whereas products such as bread and fuel will have little scope.

Now test yourself

TESTED

1 Briefly outline the difference between sales volume and sales value.
2 How is it possible for sales to increase but market share to fall?
3 Why would a business wish to achieve brand loyalty?
4 Identify three internal and three external influences on marketing objectives.
5 If XYZ plc market share is 5% and its sales are £30m, what is the total market size?

Answers on p. 115

Understanding markets and customers

The value of primary and secondary marketing research

REVISED

A market is a place where buyers and sellers come together. All businesses will sell their product or service within the relevant market. This might be direct to the consumer, online or to distributors and retailers. It is very important that a business fully understands the market in which it operates and to help with this, **market research** will be undertaken. This may involve one or more of the following:
- study of market trends and characteristics
- analysis of market shares and potential of existing products

> **Market research** is the process of gathering data on potential customers.

- sales forecasting for products
- analysis and forecasting sales of new products

Market research is separated into **primary** and **secondary research**.

Primary research

Also known as 'field research', **primary research** involves the collection of information for the first time directly by or for a business to answer specific issues or questions. Examples include:

- **Surveys:** conducting questionnaires face to face, by post, telephone or online.
- **Observation:** watching people, reactions to displays or counting footfall.
- **Focus groups:** using small groups of people to determine consumer attitudes and opinions.
- **Test marketing:** trying out products on a small group prior to a full-scale launch.

The main advantage of primary research is that it is directly related to the specific needs of a business, but it can be expensive to undertake.

> **Primary research** is the collection of information for the first time for specific purposes.

Secondary research

This is second-hand research involving the collection of data that already exists. Examples include:

- **Published reports.** These might be reports published by trade associations and journals, which may contain valuable information on markets and trends.
- **Government and other agencies.** A great deal of information is available. A key publication is the *Annual Abstract of Statistics*.
- **Internet.** Again, a great deal of information is widely available regarding markets and consumer behaviour.

Market research can also be separated into **qualitative** and **quantitative research**.

> **Secondary research** is the collection of data that already exists and has been used for other purposes.

Qualitative market research

The aim of **qualitative market research** is to find out about attitudes and opinions of consumers. It is collected from small groups of consumers such as focus groups. It can reveal consumer reactions to the:

- product
- pricing
- packaging
- branding

This might enable a business to design products that are more appealing to consumers.

> **Qualitative market research** is research into the attitudes and opinions of consumers that influence their purchasing behaviour.

Quantitative market research

Quantitative market research is the collection of information on consumer views that can be analysed statistically. It can be represented in easy-to-read charts and graphs showing:

- sales and potential sales
- size of the market
- prices consumers are prepared to pay

> **Quantitative market research** is the collection of information on consumer views and behaviour that can be analysed statistically.

Market mapping

Market mapping can enable a business to identify the position of its product in the market relative to others. Two key features of a product or service are identified, e.g. price and quality. A grid can then be established and each brand in that market can be placed on the grid according to the quality, high or low and price, high or low. Figure 3.1 is a market map of the supermarket industry. Supermarkets are placed according to price (low or high) and quality (low or high).

Figure 3.1 Market map of the UK supermarket industry

Such an approach enables a business to see where competition is most concentrated and may reveal potential gaps in the market.

The value of sampling

REVISED

A business will not collect information from all its potential consumers: this would be too expensive and time consuming. Firms need to select a sample that is representative of the whole target market (called 'the population'). **Sampling** is the selection of a representative group of consumers from a larger population. The general principle is that the larger the sample, the more accurate the results are likely to be.

There are a number of ways in which samples can be collected:

- **Random sampling.** This is when each member of the population has an equal chance of being included. This is appropriate when a firm is researching a product aimed at a large target group. Computers are often used to select people randomly.
- **Stratified random sampling.** This separates the population into segments or strata. This approach can avoid bias by ensuring that the composition of the sample reflects accurately that of the entire population.
- **Quota sampling.** This splits the population into a number of groups, each sharing common characteristics. For example, a survey might be conducted on the views of women about a new product, and the number of interviewees in each age category could be clearly set out. This saves money by limiting the number of respondents.

Factors influencing choice of sampling methods

The most obvious factor affecting the choice of sampling method is the amount of finance available. Businesses with larger marketing budgets will spend more and conduct research using larger samples.

Market research involves a fundamental trade-off between cost and accuracy. Firms require accurate information on which to base marketing decisions, such as:
- pricing policies
- product design
- types of promotion
- target customers

The greater the amount of information collected, the more reliable it should be, but the greater the cost to the firm. Many newly established businesses have limited budgets, yet accurate market research is invaluable in aiding decision-making. Firms face a further dilemma. Even extensive and costly market research cannot guarantee unbiased data. Respondents do not always tell the truth and samples do not always reflect the entire population accurately.

Exam tip

When assessing a business's methods of sampling, consider the costs of the chosen approach against the expected financial benefits.

Now test yourself

TESTED

6 List three ways primary market research differs from secondary market research.
7 Explain the difference between qualitative and quantitative market research. Support your answer with examples of situations in which they may be appropriate.
8 Briefly outline the value of sampling.

Answers on pp. 115–116

The interpretation of marketing data

REVISED

Marketing data can be interpreted using various statistical tools, including correlation, confidence intervals and extrapolation.

Correlation

Correlation occurs when there is a direct relationship between one factor and another. This relationship might be positive or negative, e.g. a price increase may lead to a fall in demand, which is a negative correlation, but a price decrease might lead to a rise in demand, which is a positive correlation. Knowledge of correlation might therefore help in decision-making, e.g. knowing that there is a positive correlation between rising incomes and sales might enable a business to more accurately forecast sales. Figures 3.2(a) and (b) illustrate positive and negative correlations.

Correlation is a statistical technique used to establish the extent of a relationship between two variables such as the level of sales and advertising.

Exam practice answers and quick quizzes at **www.hoddereducation.co.uk/myrevisionnotes**

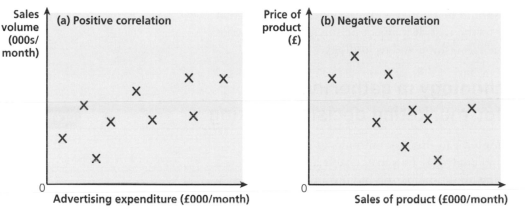

Figure 3.2 Positive and negative correlations

Figure 3.2(a) shows a positive correlation between sales and advertising expenditure and 3.2(b) a negative correlation between price and sales. Results of correlation should be treated with caution as correlation only shows a relationship between two variables. Sales might appear to rise with increased advertising, but it might be due to a competitor raising its prices rather than the increased advertising.

Confidence intervals

Since a business cannot be 100% certain in market research findings, **confidence intervals** may be used to help evaluate the reliability of any estimate. This is the **margin of error** that a researcher would experience if he/she asked a particular question to a sample group and expected to get the same answer back. For instance, if a researcher used a confidence interval of 5, and 70% of respondents gave a particular answer, then he/she could be sure that between 65% and 75% of the whole population would give the same answer.

The confidence interval used is likely to be affected by the sample size — the smaller the sample, the greater the margin for error and therefore the greater the confidence interval.

A **confidence level**, on the other hand, is an expression of how confident that researcher is in data collected. A confidence level is expressed as a percentage and indicates how frequently that percentage of the population would give an answer that would lie within the confidence interval. The most commonly used confidence level is 95%.

Extrapolation

Extrapolation uses known data to predict future data. By looking at past sales figures it may be possible to predict future sales by extending a **trend** line on a chart or graph (see Figure 3.3).

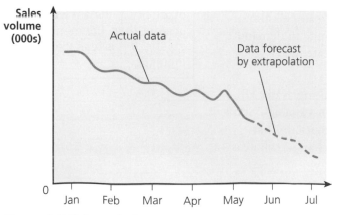

Figure 3.3 Extrapolation

> **Exam tip**
>
> Be careful with correlation. For example, just because US suicides correlate with US spending on science space and technology does not mean that there is a positive correlation.

> **Confidence interval** or **margin of error** is the plus or minus figure used to show the accuracy of results arising from sampling.
>
> **Confidence level** is the probability that research findings are correct.

> **Extrapolation** analyses past performance of a variable, such as sales, and extends the trend into the future.
>
> A **trend** is an underlying pattern of growth or decline in a series of data.

Extrapolation, however, should be treated with caution as it assumes that the future will be similar to the past. It may not be suitable for industries subject to rapid change such as fashion and technology.

The value of technology in gathering and analysing data for marketing decision-making

REVISED

Developments in technology mean that vast amounts of information can be collected, stored and analysed. This may enable a firm to gain a much greater understanding about the person buying a product and, as a result, firms such as Amazon can make recommendations to individual customers based on past buying habits.

Technology can provide faster communication, make forecasting easier, and enable targeted sales messages, but a business must have the right data in the first place.

Now test yourself

TESTED

9 Distinguish between correlation and extrapolation.
10 In market research 60% of respondents preferred a particular soap brand. What does a 5% confidence interval tell analysts about this result?

Answers on p. 116

> **Exam tip**
>
> It is important to always look critically at marketing data. At first sight it may seem reliable, but you should question whether it has been influenced by any other factors, e.g. seasonality or problems experienced by a competitor.

The interpretation of price and income elasticity of demand data

REVISED

Elasticity refers to the responsiveness of demand to a change in a variable such as price or income. The AQA specification does not require students to be able to calculate elasticity, but knowing how it is calculated can aid understanding and interpretation. The calculation for price and income elasticity are as follows:

> **Elasticity** is a measure of the responsiveness of demand to a change in a variable, e.g. price or income.

$$\text{price elasticity of demand} = \frac{\text{percentage change in demand}}{\text{percentage change in price}}$$

$$\text{income elasticity of demand} = \frac{\text{percentage change in demand}}{\text{percentage change in income}}$$

When analysing elasticity, a marketing manager will be interested in whether demand for the product or service is elastic or inelastic.

An answer greater than 1, i.e. the percentage change in demand is greater than the percentage change in the variable, indicates elastic demand. An answer less than 1, i.e. the percentage change in demand is less than the percentage change in the variable, indicates an inelastic demand.

A knowledge of elasticity can be useful in decision-making as not all products will be affected in the same way by changes in variables. Some products, e.g. bread, fuel and salt, will be relatively inelastic in that demand will change very little when price or income change, whereas others, e.g. cars and television, will be relatively elastic.

> **Exam tip**
>
> When looking at a figure for elasticity, if the answer is greater than 1 demand is elastic. If it is less than 1 it is inelastic.

The value of the concepts of price and income elasticity of demand to marketing decision-makers

REVISED

Both price and income elasticity can be useful tools in marketing decision-making. They can be used to evaluate the impact of changes in prices and incomes on sales (volume and value). The effect of changes in price is summarised in Table 3.1.

Table 3.1 The effect of changes in price

	Price rise	Price fall
Elastic demand	Total revenue falls.	Total revenue rises.
Inelastic demand	Total revenue rises.	Total revenue falls.

The impact of changes in income will vary according to the type of product. Demand for luxuries tends to be elastic, whereas demand for necessities tends to be inelastic. The demand for new cars (luxury) tends to increase with rising incomes and decrease with falling incomes, whereas the demand for fuel (necessity) is likely to be less influenced by changes in income.

Although elasticity can be a useful tool, marketing decisions should not be based on this alone. Other factors that should be considered include:
- brand loyalty
- competitor actions
- consumer tastes and fashion
- availability of substitutes

> **Exam tip**
>
> Elasticity changes over time, and it is important in decision-making to use the most up-to-date figures. A figure that is even one year old may be out of date as the market may have changed or competitors introduced new products.

The use of data in marketing decision-making and planning

REVISED

Marketing managers want to reduce risk and uncertainty in decision-making, and the analysis of all available data makes a good starting point for this. Data may also create a much better understanding of the market, environment and consumers, and so is likely to improve the quality of decision-making.

Now test yourself

TESTED

11 A business has calculated the price elasticity of its product at −2.3. What would be the impact on revenue of a price increase?
12 Briefly outline why demand for a luxury product is likely to be income elastic.

Answers on p. 116

Making marketing decisions: segmentation, targeting and positioning

Market segmentation is the process of dividing a market into distinct groups. Those customers within the same segment will share common characteristics that can help a business to target them and market to them effectively.

> **Market segmentation** is dividing the market into identifiable sub-markets, each with its own customer characteristics.

Market targeting is when a business targets its marketing at a specific market segment (or target market). Identifying the target market is an essential step in the development of a marketing plan.

Market positioning refers to how a consumer views an individual brand relative to that of competing brands. The objective of a marketing strategy may therefore be to achieve a clear, unique and therefore advantageous position in consumers' minds.

> **Market targeting** is deciding which segment a business wants to operate in.

> **Market positioning** is where a particular brand stands in relation to other brands in the market.

The process and value of segmentation, targeting and positioning

REVISED

From the above it is evident that segmentation, targeting and positioning are linked:

Segmentation ➡ Targeting ➡ Positioning

The process of segmentation breaks the market into clearly definable groups. This might be by age, gender, income, social class or geographical area. Once the market has been segmented it is then possible to determine at which groups a particular product or service will be aimed. Next, a business will consider how it wants to position its product or service within the target market. How does it want the product to be perceived by consumers? This might be in terms of its pricing, quality and overall brand image.

> **Exam tip**
>
> There is a link between market positioning and market mapping — a business might use market mapping to determine the position of its product or service in the market.

There are a number of benefits of the above process:
● Marketing will be more effective as it can be directed specifically at the target group and convey a clear message relative to the positioning of the product or service.
● Resources will be used more effectively as a result of the targeted marketing approach.
● Sales and market share may increase as a result of the clear focus of marketing.

This approach may have its drawbacks, however:
● By targeting particular segments of the market, a business may overlook a potentially profitable segment.
● It is also possible that any changes in taste and fashion could be overlooked.

Influences on choosing a target market and positioning

REVISED

There are a number of influences on the target market and positioning:
● **The nature of the product.** This might be the actual qualities of the product that help differentiate it or what the product may be used for.
● **Competition.** A business may want to avoid areas of the market that are highly competitive.
● **The consumer.** Products might be developed specifically to suit consumer needs.

One decision a business is likely to make is whether it should target a niche market or a mass market.

Niche marketing is when businesses identify and satisfy the demands of small segments of a larger market. An example is the radio station Classic

> **Niche marketing** is when businesses identify and satisfy the demands of small segments of a larger market.

FM which serves the niche of people who wish to listen to popular classical music.

The **advantages** of niche marketing are:

- The first company to identify a niche market can often gain a dominant market position as consumers become loyal to the product, even if its price is higher.
- Niche markets can be highly profitable, as companies operating in them often have the opportunity to charge premium prices.

The **disadvantages** of niche marketing are:

- Because sales may be relatively low, firms operating in niche markets may not be able to spread fixed overheads over sufficient sales to attain acceptable profit margins.
- If a niche market proves to be profitable, it is likely to attract new competition, making it less attractive to the companies that first discovered the market.

Mass marketing occurs when businesses aim their products at most of the available market. Many small and medium-sized businesses sell in mass markets.

> **Mass marketing** is when businesses aim their products at most of the available market.

Businesses must be able to produce on a large scale if they are to sell successfully in a mass market. This may mean that the firm has to invest heavily in resources such as buildings, machinery and vehicles. Often, firms have to be price competitive to flourish in mass markets, or have a unique selling point (USP) that makes the company and its products distinctive.

Now test yourself

TESTED ☐

13 Briefly outline the benefits and potential drawbacks of market targeting.
14 Distinguish between a niche and a mass market.

Answers on p. 116

Making marketing decisions: using the marketing mix

The elements of the marketing mix (7Ps)

The **marketing mix** is the combination of marketing activities that an organisation engages in so as to best meet the needs of its targeted market. The marketing mix was first developed for fast-moving consumer goods and consisted of the 4Ps of **Price, Product, Place** and **Promotion**. As the service sector has grown in importance, the mix has been expanded to include **People, Process** and **Physical environment**. It is, however, likely that all businesses will give some consideration to the three additional Ps. Figure 3.4 illustrates the mix and the aspects involved with each of the 7Ps.

> **Marketing mix** — the main variables comprising a firm's marketing strategy.

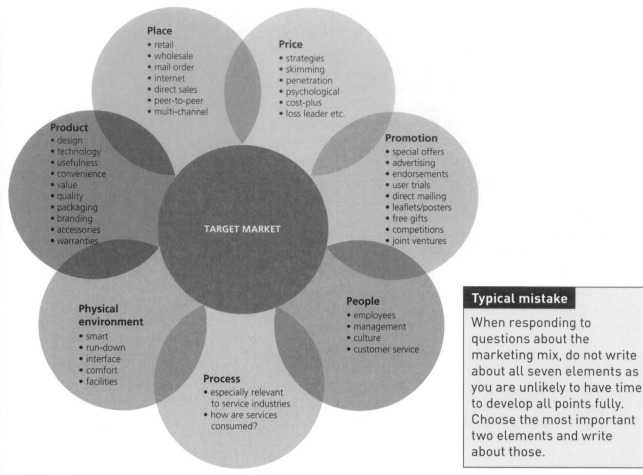

Figure 3.4 The seven Ps of marketing

The influences on and the effects of changes in the elements of the marketing mix

REVISED

Managers take a range of factors into account when designing the marketing mix for a product (see Figure 3.5).

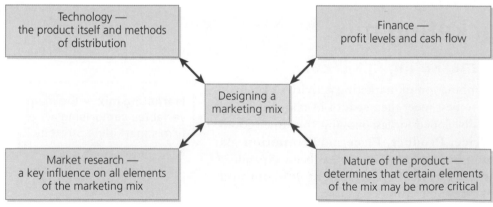

Figure 3.5 Influences on the marketing mix

Finance

The level of profits that a business earns can impact on the price that it charges. A profitable business is able to cut prices significantly, at least in the short term. Its financial reserves also enable it to engage in extensive promotional campaigns.

Exam practice answers and quick quizzes at **www.hoddereducation.co.uk/myrevisionnotes**

Another aspect of finance that affects the marketing mix is that a business with a healthy cash flow will be able to extend the range of outlets it uses by offering favourable trade credit terms.

The nature of the product

The type of product can influence which elements of the mix are emphasised. An insurance firm may spend heavily on advertising to generate large numbers of enquiries to win an acceptable number of customers. In contrast, a portrait painter may rely on the quality of the product and word-of-mouth promotion to achieve sales.

Technology

Some products that possess the latest technology may use advertising to inform potential customers of their existence and benefits. They will have high prices to maximise short-term profits and cover the costs of research and development. Technology has also affected the place element of the marketing mix. Developments have allowed publishers of music and books to distribute their products using internet downloads.

Market research

Primary market research may be the most importance influence in designing a marketing mix. Its findings may provide information to help to make judgements on the form, functions and design of the product. The research may uncover information on prices that consumers will be willing to pay and the type of purchasers. Market research may also determine pricing strategies.

> **Exam tip**
>
> When analysing the marketing mix, look carefully at the type of product. Is it being sold business to business (B2B) or business to consumer (B2C)? Is it a convenience good or a speciality good? These factors will have an influence on the marketing mix developed.

Now test yourself

TESTED

15 For what reason has the marketing mix been extended from 4Ps to 7Ps?
16 Briefly explain two factors a marketing manager will take into consideration when designing a marketing mix.

Answers on p. 116

Product decisions

REVISED

Influences on and the value of new product development

A number of factors have an effect upon the development of new goods and services:

- **Technology.** Developments in technology are at the heart of many of the new products that come on to the market. For example, advances in battery technology have helped to generate a range of more efficient electric cars. Firms use these technological advances as the basis for the development of new products that meet the needs of consumers more fully.
- **Competitors' actions.** A competitor producing a new product can be a spur to a rival to produce something that is at least as good, if not better. Hotels, for example, have improved their services by offering guests a choice of different types of pillow to enhance comfort.

- **The entrepreneurial skills of managers and owners.** One of the talents of successful entrepreneurs is creativity. The skill of being able to think up new ideas for goods and services that fit with customer needs leads to the development of many new products.

The importance of unique selling points

Businesses commonly add value by creating a **unique selling point or proposition (USP)** for their products. A USP allows a business to differentiate its products from others in the market. This can help the business in a number of ways:
- The business can base its advertising campaigns around the (real or perceived) difference between its product and those of its rivals.
- Having a USP assists in encouraging brand loyalty, as it gives customers a reason to continue to buy that particular business's product.
- A USP commonly allows the firm to charge a premium price for the product.

The product life cycle

The product life cycle is the theory that all products follow a similar pattern throughout their life. Products take varying amounts of time to pass through these stages. The Mars Bar was launched in the 1920s and is still going strong. In contrast, modern motor cars are expected to have a life cycle of about 10 years. The stages are outlined below and illustrated in Figure 3.6.

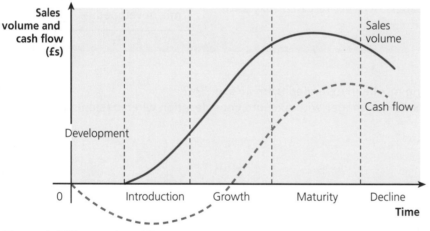

Figure 3.6 The product life cycle

1 **Development.** Firms undertake research and development to create new products that will be their future best sellers. Many products fall by the wayside, as they do not meet the demands of consumers. This can be a very expensive stage and cash flow is expected to be negative.
2 **Introduction.** This stage commences with the product's initial appearance on the market. At this time, sales are zero and the product has a negative cash flow. Sales should begin to rise, providing the company with some revenue. However, costs will remain high. The failure rate for new products is high — 60% to 90%. Promotion can be expensive and cash flow will remain negative. The price may have to be high to recoup the high initial launch costs.

A **unique selling point or proposition (USP)** allows a business to differentiate its products from others in the market.

3 **Growth.** During the growth stage, sales rise rapidly and a firm's cash flow can improve considerably. The business's profits per unit sold are likely to be at a maximum. This is because firms tend to charge a high price at this stage, particularly if the product is innovatory. Firms with a technically superior good may well engage in price skimming (see p. 47). The growth stage is critical to a product's survival. The product's success will depend on how competitors react to it.

4 **Maturity.** During the maturity stage, the sales curve peaks and begins to decline. Both cash flow and profits also decline. This stage is characterised by intense competition with other brands. Competitors emphasise improvements and differences in their versions of the product. At this stage, consumers of the product know a lot about it and require specialist deals to attract their interest.

5 **Decline.** During the decline stage, sales fall rapidly. New technology or a new product change may cause product sales to decline sharply. When this happens, marketing managers consider eliminating unprofitable products. At this stage, promotional efforts will be cut too.

Extension strategies

Firms may attempt to prolong the life of a product as it enters the decline stage by implementing extension strategies. They may use techniques such as the following:

- **Finding new markets for existing products.** Some companies selling baby milk have targeted less economically developed countries.
- **Changing the appearance or packaging.** Some motor manufacturers have produced old models of cars with new colours or other features to extend the lives of their products.

The product mix

A well-organised business will plan its product range so that it has products in each of the major stages of the life cycle: as one product reaches decline, replacements are entering the growth and maturity stages of their lives (see Figure 3.7). This means that there will be a constant flow of income from products in the mature phase of their lives to finance the development of new products.

Exam tip

For all major theories, such as the product life cycle, you should be able to give some assessment of the theory's strengths and weaknesses. This will help you to write evaluatively as well as confirming your understanding.

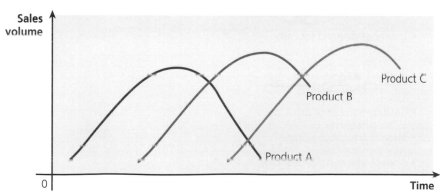

Figure 3.7 A healthy product mix

The Boston matrix

The Boston matrix was developed by the Boston Consulting Group. The matrix allows businesses to undertake product portfolio analysis based on the product's market growth rate and its market share.

The matrix, as shown in Figures 3.8 and 3.9, places products into four categories:

- **Star products** have a dominant share of the market and good prospects for growth.
- **Cash cows** are products with a dominant share of the market but low prospects for growth.
- **Dogs** have a low share of the market and no prospects for growth.
- **Problem children** are products that have a small share of a growing market.

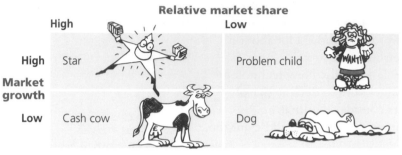

Figure 3.8 The Boston matrix

A number of conclusions can be drawn from the Boston matrix:

- Firms should avoid having too many products in any single category. Obviously, firms do not want lots of dogs, but they also need to avoid having too many stars and problem children.
- Products in the top half of the chart are in the early stages of their life cycle and are in growing markets, but the cost of developing and promoting them will not have been recovered.
- Continuing production of cash cows will provide the necessary cash to develop the newer products.
- Firms need problem child products as they may become tomorrow's cash cows.

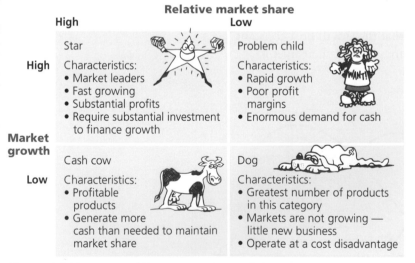

Figure 3.9 Features of the components of the marketing mix

Now test yourself

TESTED

17 Briefly explain the difference between the Boston matrix and product life cycle and suggest how managers might use them to make decisions about the portfolio of products being sold.
18 Explain the difference between a cash cow and problem child in the Boston matrix.

Answers on p. 116

Exam practice answers and quick quizzes at **www.hoddereducation.co.uk/myrevisionnotes**

Pricing decisions

The pricing strategies used by businesses

The **price of a product** is simply the amount that a business expects a customer to pay to purchase the good or service.

Pricing strategies are the medium- to long-term pricing plans that a business adopts. There are four principal pricing strategies:

1 **Price skimming.** This is often used when a new, innovative product is launched. It is unlikely that this product will face direct competition immediately. By setting a high price, the business will achieve limited sales but with a high profit margin on each. This allows the firm to recoup some of the product's development costs. The price is lowered when competitors enter the market.

2 **Penetration pricing.** Firms entering a market with products similar to those already available may use penetration pricing. The price is set deliberately low to gain a foothold in the market. The expectation is that, once the product is established, the price will be increased to boost profit margins.

3 **Price leadership.** Price leadership is used for established products with strong brand images. The firm adopting this strategy will probably dominate the market and other businesses will usually follow their lead.

4 **Price taking.** Price takers set their prices equal to the 'going rate' or the established market price. This is a common pricing strategy for small and medium-sized businesses. Price takers have no influence over the market price, as they are normally one of many smallish firms competing for business.

Once a business has determined its pricing strategy, it may employ a number of pricing tactics. Pricing tactics are a series of pricing techniques that are normally used only over the short term to achieve specific goals. They include:

● **Loss leaders.** This entails setting prices very low (often below the cost of production) to attract customers. Businesses using this tactic hope that customers will purchase other (full-price) products while purchasing the loss leader.

● **Special-offer pricing.** This approach involves reduced prices for a limited period of time or offers such as 'three for the price of two'.

Influences on pricing decisions

There is a range of factors that might influence a firm in its pricing decisions. A firm is more likely to select strategies and tactics that result in low prices if it is seeking to expand its market share. This type of approach may also be more popular with businesses that are in a financially strong position. In contrast, a business that is selling a product that is highly differentiated or facing increasing popularity may opt for higher price levels.

Price elasticity of demand

One key factor influencing managers in their pricing decisions is price elasticity of demand. **Price elasticity of demand** measures the extent to which the level of demand for a product is sensitive to price changes. An increase in price is almost certain to reduce demand, while a price reduction can be expected to increase the level of demand. However,

> **Price of a product** — the amount that a business expects a customer to pay to purchase the good or service.
>
> **Pricing strategies** — the medium- to long-term pricing plans that a business adopts.

> **Typical mistake**
>
> Some students write about pricing tactics when the question asks about pricing strategies. If a question asks about strategies, you must write about relevant pricing actions that a business can take in the long term, and not short-term tactical decisions.

> **Price elasticity of demand** is the extent to which the level of demand for a product is sensitive to price changes.

the extent to which demand changes following a given price change is less predictable.

Demand is said to be price elastic if it is sensitive to price changes. So, an increase in price will result in a significant lowering of demand and a fall in the firm's revenue. Products with a lot of competition are price elastic, as an increase in price will result in substantial loss of sales.

Price inelastic demand exists when price changes have relatively little effect on the level of demand. Examples of products with price inelastic demand are petrol and other essentials. Price elasticity of demand (PED) is calculated by the formula:

$$\text{price elasticity of demand} = \frac{\text{percentage change in quantity demanded}}{\text{percentage change in price}}$$

Firms would prefer to sell products with demand that is price inelastic, as this gives greater freedom in selecting a pricing strategy and more opportunity to raise prices, total revenue and profits.

Businesses can adopt a number of techniques to make demand for their products more price inelastic:

● **Differentiating products from those of competitors.** Making a product significantly different from those of competitors can increase brand loyalty. Consumers are more likely to continue to purchase a product when its price rises if it has unique characteristics.
● **Reducing competition through takeovers and mergers.** In recent years, many markets have seen fewer, but larger firms competing with each other. This process results in fewer products being available to the consumer and may mean that demand will be less responsive to price.

Now test yourself

TESTED

19 Using examples, explain the difference between a pricing strategy and a pricing tactic.
20 Outline the circumstances in which a business might decide to use a strategy of price skimming.

Answers on p. 116

Decisions about the promotional mix

REVISED

What is promotion?

Promotion is bringing consumers' attention to a product or business. Promotion aims to achieve targets including:

● to attract new customers and retain existing customers
● to improve the position of the business in the market
● to ensure the survival and growth of the business
● to increase awareness of a product

> **Promotion** is bringing consumers' attention to a product or business.

Exam tip

It is easy to think that promotion just means advertising. Figure 3.10 emphasises that this is not the case. Strong answers to examination questions on this topic will demonstrate awareness of the circumstances in which each of the elements of the promotional mix might be appropriate.

The elements of the promotional mix

The **promotional mix** is the combination of methods used by businesses to communicate with prospective customers to inform them of their products and to persuade them to buy these products.

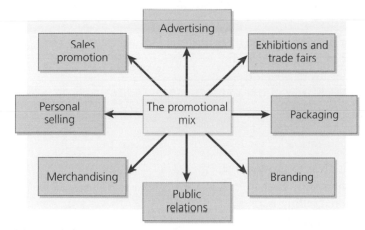

Figure 3.10 The promotional mix

Promotional mix — the combination of methods used by businesses to communicate with prospective customers to inform them of their products and to persuade them to buy these products.

Advertising

Advertising is a paid form of non-personal communication using mass media to change the attitudes and buying behaviour of consumers. Advertising can be separated into two types:
- **Informative advertising.** This is designed to increase consumer awareness of a product by providing consumers with factual information. Such adverts centre on the prices and features of the products being advertised.
- **Persuasive advertising.** This attempts to get consumers to purchase a particular product by, for example, claiming that the product is better than the competition.

Advertising is a paid form of non-personal communication using mass media to change the attitudes and buying behaviour of consumers

Sales promotions and merchandising

Merchandising is in-store promotional activity by manufacturers or retailers at the point of sale. Merchandising can be important when consumers make purchasing decisions at the point of sale and a variety of rival products are on display in stores — confectionery is an example.

Other forms of sales promotion include:
- special offers and competitions
- in-store demonstrations
- coupons, vouchers and free gifts

These forms of promotion may be used when rival businesses wish to avoid starting a price war, which they might not win. Merchandising can be relatively cheap, but is not good at targeting specific groups of consumers.

Packaging

Packaging emphasises the attractiveness of the product and informs consumers of its features, functions and contents. Packaging also protects the good during its distribution to ensure that it reaches the consumer in perfect condition.

Exhibitions and trade fairs

These are events staged to attract all those people involved in a particular market, both sellers and buyers. An example is the Motor Show held in Birmingham each year.

Branding

This establishes an identity for a product that distinguishes it from the competition. Successful branding allows higher prices to be charged and can extend the product's life cycle by creating customer loyalty. Brand loyalty occurs when consumers regularly purchase particular products and it can allow firms to charge higher prices.

Personal selling

Personal selling involves visits by a firm's sales representatives to prospective customers. This may be used more in business-to-business selling, or in selling expensive products such as double glazing. Personal selling is a relatively expensive method of raising public awareness of a product.

Public relations (PR)

PR is promoting the company's image to establish a favourable public attitude towards the company. It aims to improve the image of a business and its products in the expectation of increasing sales through sponsoring sporting or cultural activities or making donations to worthwhile causes.

Influences on the choice of promotional mix

Managers will take into account a range of factors when deciding on the precise promotional mix to be deployed:

- **The product's position in its life cycle.** A newly launched product is likely to need heavy advertising to inform customers of its existence and the benefits it provides. An established product may use sales promotions to persuade customers to buy it.
- **The type of product.** Expensive products and those where design is a major element will make greater use of exhibitions and trade fairs in the promotional mix. This element of the mix is important, for example, to firms selling homes and fashion products.
- **The finance available to the business.** Firms with larger budgets may engage more in public relations and personal selling, as these methods of promotion are expensive.
- **Where consumers make purchasing decisions.** For businesses that sell products that are purchased on impulse, often at the point of sale, merchandising and packaging may be particularly important. The attractiveness of the wrappers and the positioning of the product within shops may be vital.
- **Competitors' actions.** If a business's rivals are engaging in heavy advertising or extensive sales promotions, it is likely that the business will respond similarly. This is more likely if the business trades in a market where there is relatively little product differentiation.

> **Typical mistake**
>
> Many students respond to questions about the promotional mix by writing about the marketing mix. Do not confuse these two concepts.

Now test yourself

TESTED

21 State four elements of the promotional mix.
22 Explain two influences on the promotional mix of a newly opened restaurant.

Answers on p. 116

Exam practice answers and quick quizzes at **www.hoddereducation.co.uk/myrevisionnotes**

Distribution (place) decisions

The **distribution of a product** refers to the range of activities necessary to make the product available to customers.

Choosing appropriate outlets and distributors

The choice of an outlet or a distributor to supply the products to outlets must fit with the rest of the product's marketing mix. For example, it is vital that if the product is to be sold cheaply, possibly to increase market share, then suitable outlets are chosen. In this situation, a cost-cutting retail outlet might be appropriate, so that the benefit of low prices is passed on to the final customer.

Other factors that a business might take into account when choosing outlets and distributors include:
- **Location.** Businesses will seek outlets and distributors in areas where their target customers live and where few competitors operate.
- **Credit terms.** A newly established or struggling enterprise might opt for outlets or distributors that do not request long periods of trade credit. This can help to protect a business's cash flow.
- **Willingness to display products in prominent positions.** For some products (e.g. foods and confectionery), a good position in a retail outlet is an essential part of successful distribution.

The types of distribution channel that exist

There are a number of different forms of distribution. The three main channels are illustrated in Figure 3.11.
- **Traditional.** Many small retailers buy stock from wholesalers, as they do not purchase sufficient quantities to buy directly from producers. Wholesalers offer other benefits besides small quantities, such as advice, credit and delivery, although they can be expensive.
- **Modern.** Major retailers such as Marks and Spencer purchase directly from manufacturers and arrange their own distribution. They can do this because they buy huge quantities of products and are able to negotiate large discounts that more than cover the costs of distribution. As a consequence, they can offer discounts to consumers, enhancing their market position.
- **Direct.** This is a rapidly growing channel of distribution. It is attractive to many firms because it lowers the prices at which they can sell products to the consumer. Many small businesses have started to sell their products directly to customers using the internet.

> **Distribution of a product**
> involves the range of activities necessary to make the product available to customers.

> **Typical mistake**
> Do not ignore place or distribution. It is sometimes called 'the forgotten P' and students often respond poorly to questions that are set on it. You should know the different distribution methods and which are appropriate in different circumstances.

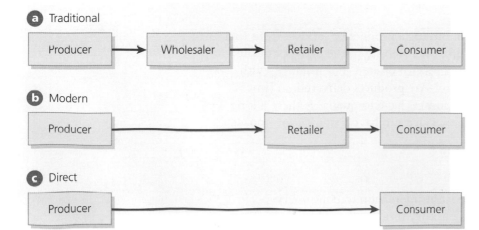

Figure 3.11 The channels of distribution

The choice of a distribution channel will be influenced by a number of factors:

- **The type of product.** Products that are difficult to transport because of their bulk, fragility or perishable nature are more likely to be distributed direct to avoid incurring additional costs. Producers selling large amounts of relatively low-priced products are more likely to use a wholesaler as it is expensive to store this type of product.
- **The nature of the market.** Businesses selling in dispersed markets usually require the services of wholesalers as they have the resources to supply in these circumstances.
- **The technical complexity of the product.** Technically complex products (such as laptops) are better distributed when the customer and the producer can easily contact each other to solve problems of installation or operation.

Multi-channel distribution

Consumers today expect to be able to access products in a variety of ways: in shops, online and click and collect. As a result many businesses now offer **multi-channel distribution**.

> **Multi-channel distribution**
> — where firms use more then one type of distribution channel.

Now test yourself

TESTED

23 Tesco uses a multi-channel distribution strategy. Briefly outline the different channels it uses.

Answer on p. 116

Decisions relating to other elements of the marketing mix: people, process and physical environment

REVISED

People

The people involved with selling a service or a product are crucial and can make or break a sale. A customer's first impressions of a business are important and it is essential that the people offering advice or delivering the service are interested, helpful and polite. It is therefore important that employees are well trained and motivated, as good customer service can enhance a business's reputation, sometimes providing a USP and increased brand loyalty.

Process

This relates to the whole process of buying a product or service, from first entering a business premises or going on a website to the delivery of the product or service and the after-sales service offered. For instance, with online sales, is the website easy to use? Are products delivered on time? Or for a fast food restaurant, do consumers have to queue? Is there a long wait for food? The efficiency of the service can have a significant impact on the level of sales.

Physical environment

It is important a business gives the right impression to consumers. The premises of a business selling a luxury product should be located in a more up-market area and the decor should reflect the nature of the product.

Now test yourself

TESTED

24 Briefly explain why people and process are just as important when selling products as they are for selling services.

Answer on p. 116

The importance of and the influences on an integrated marketing mix

REVISED

The importance of an integrated marketing mix

An integrated marketing mix is one that fits together. If a business is selling a premium product, the entire mix should support this. The elements might be constructed as follows:

- **Product.** This should be high quality in terms of design, innovativeness, features or functions.
- **Price.** The price is likely to be high (skimming) to reflect the premium nature of the product.
- **Place.** The business would seek outlets that reflect the quality or exclusivity of the product.
- **Promotion.** This would be targeted at the people who are likely to purchase the product.
- **Physical environment** should reflect the premium nature of the product. **People** should be well trained and motivated in order to deliver the customer service necessary for a more exclusive premium product. Consumers should find the whole **process** from first deciding to purchase to the delivery of the product or service first rate.

If the marketing mix is inconsistent, consumers may be deterred from purchasing the product, thereby depressing sales and profits. In the case of a premium product, a low price might be a mistake as it may lead some consumers to think that the product is not premium quality.

> **Exam tip**
>
> Remember that marketing mixes can be integrated in different ways depending on factors such as price and the target audience. For example, easyJet and Rolls Royce have markedly different marketing mixes, but both are integrated.

Influences on an integrated marketing mix

There are a number of influences on an integrated marketing mix:

- **Position in the product life cycle.** A product in the growth stage will need a different mix to one in the maturity or decline stage.
- **Boston matrix.** A cash cow will require a very different mix to a problem child.
- **Type of product.** The type of product and where it is sold, for example a product that is sold business to business (B2B), will require a different mix to one that is sold business to consumer (B2C).
- **Marketing objectives.** The mix is likely to change with changes in marketing objectives. For example if an objective of growth is introduced this might require additional promotion and adjustments to place.
- **Target market.** The mix should reflect the target market. For example, younger buyers may be more in tune with online sales than older buyers.

- **Competition.** Businesses should be looking to stay ahead of competitors; reviewing and changing the mix may enable them to achieve this.
- **Positioning.** The mix should reflect the positioning in the market, for instance whether it is a convenience or a luxury good.

Now test yourself

TESTED

25 Briefly explain how positioning and product life cycle might affect the marketing mix.

Answer on p. 116

Understanding the value of digital marketing and e-commerce

REVISED

Developments in technology have had a significant impact on the business marketing function. Benefits include:
- Businesses can gather more detailed information about consumers and build relationships with them. This is illustrated by the way in which Amazon continuously recommends products based on past shopping purchases.
- There is greater contact between consumer and business, allowing consumers to build their own products and give reviews of products or services purchased.
- Social media has also become very important and cannot be underestimated from a business point of view. If a business can tap into this with its marketing it can be a very cost-effective way of boosting sales.
- Digital marketing makes it easy for any business to set up and sell almost anywhere in the world.

Exam tip

Although there are many positives associated with digital marketing it is important to remember there are some negatives. Reputations can be destroyed through online reviews and social media. Consumers are free to write reviews on products and services which may not always be a true reflection of the product or service offered.

Now test yourself

TESTED

26 Briefly explain how digital marketing has benefited businesses.

Answer on p. 116

Exam practice

JJ's plc

JJ's plc is a manufacturer of a range of soft drinks targeted at a variety of markets and age groups within the mass market. Its latest product, branded JJ's Fitness Fuel, failed to generate forecast target sales. This was despite extensive primary market research, which included both qualitative and quantitative research. The qualitative research in particular indicated that consumers liked the product. Market mapping also indicated a gap in the market for an essentially healthy fitness drink. Jim Jones, managing director, was unsure of the next move. What he did know, however, was that his business needed a new rising star in its product portfolio and not a dog.

The latest brainstorming session about the product raised the following questions:
● Had JJ's put too much emphasis on product in the marketing mix?
● Is it targeting the wrong market?

Fit people tend to be healthy, so the product might not appeal. Should JJ's target a wider market and reposition the product? Should it change the marketing mix, particularly price, which was set slightly higher, and should it aim for a much wider distribution?

Questions
a What do you understand by the terms rising star and dog in the Boston matrix?   [4]
b Explain the various forms of qualitative market research JJ's might have used.   [6]
c Analyse the possible drawbacks to JJ's of targeting a narrow market segment.   [9]
d To what extent do you believe JJ's may have put too much emphasis on product in its
   marketing mix?   [16]

Answers and quick quiz 3 online

ONLINE

Summary

You should now have an understanding of all the points below.

Setting marketing objectives
● the value of setting and the internal and external influences on marketing objectives

Understanding markets and customers
● the value of primary (including sampling) and secondary market research
● the calculation of market and sales growth, market share and size
● the interpretation of marketing data including correlation and extrapolation
● the value and interpretation of price and income elasticity
● the use of data in marketing decision-making and the value of technology in this

Making marketing decisions: segmentation, targeting and positioning
● the process and value of segmentation, targeting and positioning

● influences on choosing a target market and positioning including niche and mass marketing

Making marketing decisions: using the marketing mix
● the 7Ps of the marketing mix, influences on and effects of changes in them
● product decisions including Boston matrix, product life cycle and new product development
● pricing decisions including penetration and skimming
● promotional mix decisions
● decisions related to people, process and physical environment
● the importance of an integrated marketing mix
● value of digital marketing and e-commerce

4 Decision-making to improve operational performance

The operations function of a business is the function that is responsible for the actual production of a good or service. It involves managing the process of transforming inputs into outputs. An important concept in this process is that of **added value**. This means the value of the final output, product or service, will be greater than the value of all the inputs added together. Adding value therefore enables a profit to be made and is likely to be an operational target.

> **Added value** is an amount added to the value of a product or service, equal to the difference between its cost and the amount received when it is sold.

> **Exam tip**
>
> It is not only the operations process that can add value. Marketing can also create greater brand awareness and a USP, which will add value in terms of a higher selling price.

Setting operational objectives

The value of setting operational objectives

`REVISED`

Besides added value, operational objectives might include the following:
- **Costs.** Anything a business can do to lower costs is likely to improve competitiveness. In terms of operations management objectives this will relate to unit costs of production. These might be reduced by achieving greater capacity utilisation or improved productivity, or by negotiating better terms with suppliers.
- **Quality.** If a business can consistently provide a quality product or service, this is likely to lead to a competitive advantage. Quality, however, is more than just the final product or service. It involves the whole process of operations. Targets in quality could therefore be set for any of the following: wastage, returns, number of complaints and reliability.
- **Speed of response and flexibility.** This is the time taken for a customer need to be fulfilled, e.g. the time taken from ordering a meal in a restaurant to receiving it or from ordering a product online to receiving it. The time taken will impact on the customer's perception of a business and in turn on reputation and sales. It is therefore important that if any targets are set in this respect they are met.
- **Dependability.** This relates to the reliability of a business in terms of product and service. Is a product reliable? Is quality consistent? Does a business do what it says it will do, e.g. is first class post delivered the next day? Failure in this objective is likely to damage a business's reputation and lead to a loss of sales.
- **Environmental objectives.** With greater consumer awareness, environmental objectives have taken on a much greater importance over recent years. Examples in this area could relate to pollution, minimising waste, the amount of packaging used, recycling and sustainability.

Whatever the operational objectives, they must fit with the overall corporate objectives and, as with all objectives, they must be SMART. By being SMART they can be used to evaluate and judge the overall performance of operations management.

External and internal influences on operational objectives

Like other functional areas, the operations function does not operate in isolation. Internally, any decision made will have implications for the other functional areas in a business, and externally the environment a business operates in will be changing all the time.

External influences

Operational decisions will be affected by the following external influences:

- **Political or legal influences.** Businesses always have to be aware of the legal environment and potential changes in legislation both from government and, in the case of EU, countries from the EU. This is illustrated by the greater awareness in recent years of health and safety and environmental issues, which has brought increasing amounts of legislation.
- **Economic influences.** The operations function needs to be both prepared for and respond to changes in the economy as demand will fluctuate according to the stage of the **economic cycle**. In addition, due to the global nature of the economy, resources can be sourced from anywhere in the world and it is possible to undertake production from anywhere, both factors that may be considered by the operations function.
- **Technological influences.** Technology has had a significant impact on the operations function both in terms of production and the way consumers purchase goods and services. The introduction of computer aided design (CAD) and computer aided manufacture (CAM) has resulted in speedier innovation and production and better quality. The advent of the internet means that consumers are more aware and demanding in terms of price, quality and customer service. Newspapers can be read online and books, films and music can be simply downloaded by consumers. There are apps for just about anything, and the growth of social media has an influence on operational objectives.
- **Competitive influences.** Markets have become increasingly competitive with competition both at home and from overseas. As a result, there is increasing pressure on businesses in terms of costs, quality and price. Added to this is a greater awareness amongst consumers resulting in increasing pressure on the operations function to play its part in maintaining consumer loyalty.

> The **economic cycle** is the natural fluctuation of the economy between periods of expansion (growth) and contraction (recession).

Internal influences

- **Finance.** The availability of finance will determine the extent of any operational decision-making, e.g. investment in new production technology.
- **Marketing.** It is likely that the marketing function will determine both what has to be produced and the quantities, so the operations department will have to liaise closely with the marketing department.
- **Human resources.** The skills of the workforce determine both what can be produced and its quality.

The above illustrates the integrated nature of a business, and the operations manager needs to analyse the impact of any decision on each functional area. Added to this will be the awareness of the overall corporate objectives as these are likely to be the drivers of decision-making.

> **Exam tip**
>
> When analysing and evaluating the influences on decision-making, your aim should be to identify which factors are most important and why for the business in the question.

4 Decision-making to improve operational performance

Analysing operational performance

Included under the heading of operations data are four main areas:

- capacity
- capacity utilisation
- labour productivity
- unit costs

A business is likely to set targets in each of these areas. Any targets set will be SMART and can be used to identify trends and judge performance.

Calculation of operations data

REVISED

Capacity

When referring to the capacity of a business we are referring to the total or maximum amount a business can produce in a given time period if it is working flat out.

Capacity utilisation

Capacity utilisation refers to the actual production of a business in a given time period as a percentage of the maximum capacity and is calculated as follows:

$$\frac{\text{actual output in time period}}{\text{maximum possible output per period}} \times 100$$

For example, if a business has a maximum capacity of 10,000 units and is producing 7,500 units, its capacity utilisation is 75%:

$$\frac{7,500}{10,000} \times 100 = 75\%$$

> **Capacity utilisation** measures the extent to which a business uses its production potential. It is usually expressed as a percentage.

Labour productivity

Labour productivity relates to the efficiency of individual workers and is of interest to human resources as well as operational managers. Put simply, it is a measure of the output per worker in a given time period. It is calculated as follows:

$$\text{labour productivity} = \frac{\text{output per time period}}{\text{number of employees}}$$

If in the example above the business employed 75 workers, the labour productivity would be 100 units per worker:

$$\frac{7,500}{75} = 100 \text{ units per worker}$$

> **Labour productivity** measures the output per worker in a given time period.

Unit cost

This is sometimes referred to as the 'average cost of production' and is the cost of producing one unit of output. It is calculated as follows:

$$\frac{\text{total cost}}{\text{units of output}}$$

Using the example above, again if total costs were £150,000, **unit costs** would be £20:

$$\frac{£150,000}{7,500} = £20$$

> **Unit cost** is the cost of producing one unit (item) of a good or service.

The interpretation and use of data in operational decision-making and planning

REVISED

There are a number of points to note from looking at data in operational decision-making and planning. If capacity utilisation goes up, labour productivity will rise (assuming the number employed remains the same). In addition, unit cost of production will be reduced, as the fixed costs will be spread over more units of output. If capacity utilisation decreases, the opposite will occur — labour productivity will decline (assuming the number employed remains the same) and unit costs will increase, as fixed costs are now spread over fewer units of output.

A change in the number employed will also impact on productivity. If a business can maintain a certain level of output with fewer employees, the productivity of the remainder will rise. Employing more workers without increasing output would lead to a decline in productivity.

A knowledge of operational data is therefore key when making operational decisions and planning.

Now test yourself

TESTED

3 Distinguish between capacity and capacity utilisation.
4 A business has a maximum capacity of 25,000 units and currently produces 20,000 units with 75 employees. Total costs of production are £1m. Calculate capacity utilisation, labour productivity and unit costs of production.
5 Explain why unit costs of production will decline when capacity utilisation and labour productivity increase.

Answers on p. 117

Making operational decisions to improve performance: increasing efficiency and productivity

Increasing operational efficiency is all about getting more output from a given level of resources. If this can be achieved, then unit costs will fall, enabling a business to charge more competitive prices. There are a number of aspects related to improving efficiency and these are investigated below.

The importance of capacity

Capacity and the level of capacity utilisation are very important to operational efficiency. We have already seen that unit costs decline as capacity utilisation increases. It is therefore important that a business does not have too much spare or **excess capacity**. Operating at 60% capacity utilisation results in 40% spare or excess capacity, which means that resources in terms of factory space, equipment and possibly labour are not being used efficiently. On the other hand, operating at maximum capacity would create its own problems as this would reduce flexibility in terms of new orders. It might also put undue pressure on workers and machinery if proper maintenance could not be undertaken. It is therefore important that a business operates at an **optimal level of capacity**, i.e. as close to 100% as possible, whilst leaving sufficient spare capacity to cope with new orders. In a growing market this would need to be planned carefully.

> **Excess capacity** occurs where actual production falls below maximum potential production.

> **Exam tip**
>
> When making a judgement about an individual business's capacity utilisation, it is important to compare with both capacity utilisation in previous years and the average for that industry.

The importance of efficiency and labour productivity

Labour productivity is a measure of output per worker in a given time period. An increase in labour productivity is likely to lead to a reduction in the unit costs of production and therefore could lead to a business being more competitive in terms of price.

How to increase efficiency and labour productivity

The following methods might be used to increase efficiency and labour productivity:

- **Investment in technology.** Such investment may both improve the quality and reliability of a product and result in greater output from fewer employees.
- **Improvements in training and motivation.** The aim of training is to improve the skills of the workforce, which is likely to lead to greater output. In addition, if as a result of training employees feel more involved in the process, this could lead to greater motivation and further improvements in both quality and output.
- **Job redesign.** This involves changing the content of a job in terms of duties and responsibilities and may be executed in such a way as to improve the overall performance of the employee in question.
- **Reduction in the labour force.** A reduction of the labour force will automatically improve productivity if the same level of output can be maintained. This might be achieved through investment in technology or better training.

> **Exam tip**
>
> It is important to recognise that improvements in productivity should come without any reduction in quality or dependability of service.

For more on job design, training and motivation see the human resources section on pp. 98–110.

The benefits and difficulties of lean production

Lean production is all about getting more from less. It is a Japanese approach to management that focuses on cutting out waste in terms of time, space and resources. Features of lean production include just-in-time (JIT) management, Kaizen, total quality management (TQM) and quality circles, and it is the first of these that is included in the AQA AS specification.

Just-in-time management (JIT)

Just-in-time management is an inventory (stock) strategy companies employ to increase efficiency and decrease waste by receiving goods only when they are needed in the production process. The benefits of such a system is that it reduces waste in terms of damaged stock or stock going out of date, and reduces the amount of space needed as there is no requirement for storage warehouses. It may also save time and reduce the number of employees required as the stock will be delivered directly to the production line. Less waste, space, time and employees will result in lower costs and help to improve the competitiveness of a business.

Further benefits might be greater flexibility as a business may be able to respond more quickly to changing customer tastes and needs. Additionally, there may be a reduced likelihood of being left with outdated, unsold stock. JIT also requires a much greater involvement from the workforce in terms of ensuring production continues uninterrupted, leading to greater responsibility and potential improvements in motivation.

For more on employee engagement see pp. 104–110.

Despite the many benefits, JIT does have a number of **drawbacks**:

- **Running out of stock.** JIT relies on the supplier delivering on time. Any transport problems due to weather or industrial action could halt production. In addition, if supplier firms are struck by disaster, as happened in Japan with the earthquake and tsunami in 2011, production can be interrupted for months.
- **Opportunities for bulk purchase.** Supplies will be purchased in smaller quantities and only when needed, and this may limit the opportunity for bulk purchase discounts.
- **Trust.** Such a system is dependent on the relationship between the company and its supplier. A company must have complete trust in the supplier to provide the necessary quality required as components will be going straight onto the production line.

> **Just-in-time management (JIT)** is an inventory strategy companies employ to increase efficiency and decrease waste by receiving goods only as they are needed for production.

> **Typical mistake**
>
> Although it is possible that the opportunity to benefit from bulk purchase discounts may be lost when using a JIT strategy, a business may be able to negotiate a special price for buying on-going supplies over a period of time. This is because the supplier will also save costs due to the reduced requirement for storage and themselves undertaking JIT production.

> **Now test yourself**
>
> TESTED
>
> 6 Briefly outline two advantages and two disadvantages of JIT production.
>
> Answer on p. 117

Difficulties of increasing efficiency and labour productivity

REVISED

The difficulties of increasing efficiency and labour productivity include:

- **Cost.** Any improvement in labour productivity is likely to come with a cost. New technology is expensive, and workers who have been trained and acquired new skills may demand higher pay. However, improvements in productivity may lead to greater competitiveness and greater sales, which in the long run may more than cover the original costs.

- **Quality.** When looking to improve labour productivity, a business needs to make sure this is not achieved at the expense of lower quality. This can be the case when workers are encouraged to produce more through financial incentives, e.g. working on a piece-rate system.
- **Resistance of employees.** Sometimes employees can be resistant to change, especially where job losses are concerned and job security is threatened. The introduction of technology into the production process often brings with it job losses, and a business would need to consider carefully how it is introduced.

> **Exam tip**
>
> Whether to adopt a long- or a short-term approach to improving labour productivity lends itself to evaluation.

Now test yourself

TESTED

7 Draw up a table to show the benefits and drawbacks of investing in improving labour productivity.

Answer on p. 117

How to choose the optimal mix of resources

REVISED

Resources are the factors of production:
- **land:** physical land and the natural resources, e.g. oil and iron ore
- **labour:** the workers employed by a business
- **capital:** the machines and equipment used in a business
- **enterprise:** the skill of combining the other factors of production

The requirements for these resources will vary from one business to another and will depend on the nature of the business and what it can afford. A business operating in the service sector, for instance, will have different requirements to one operating in manufacturing.

In addition, what might be an optimal mix for one business might be different for another even though they are operating in the same industry. For instance, some businesses may employ a **capital-intensive** approach to production where there is a high level of capital equipment used and a lower emphasis on labour. Other businesses might be more **labour intensive**, placing a greater emphasis on labour and less on capital equipment. A capital-intensive approach to manufacturing might be employed in countries where labour is expensive, and a labour-intensive approach where labour is relatively cheap. It is also the case that some industries, such as oil refineries and chemical plants, by their very nature are likely to be capital intensive, whereas others, such as hotels or restaurants, are more likely to be labour intensive.

> **Capital intensive** describes those businesses requiring a large amount of capital relative to labour.
>
> **Labour intensive** describes those businesses requiring a large proportion of labour relative to capital.

Now test yourself

TESTED

8 Explain the likely benefits to a company manufacturing in the UK of a capital-intensive approach to production.

Answer on p. 117

How to utilise capacity efficiently

Achieving the optimum level of capacity utilisation is very important. In order to overcome situations of excess or spare capacity a business might consider the following:

- **Increase sales.** This might be achieved by undertaking a new marketing campaign or introducing extension strategies to find new uses or markets for a product.
- **Reduce capacity.** If a low level of capacity utilisation is expected to continue far into the future, it might be advisable to rationalise production and sell off some capacity. Such a decision should not be taken lightly as once done it cannot be reversed.
- **Alternative uses.** It may be possible to find alternative uses for the capacity, such as the introduction of new products or leasing it to other businesses.

If demand is so high that a business is facing the problem of lack of capacity it might consider the following:

- **Outsourcing.** This involves transferring portions of work to outside suppliers.
- **Investment.** This involves investment into the permanent establishment of new capacity, but should only be undertaken if high levels of demand are expected to continue well into the future.
- **Reducing demand.** This might be achieved by increasing price. The use of **dynamic pricing** has enabled businesses, such as airlines and hotels, to control more effectively the level of demand.

> **Dynamic pricing** is a pricing strategy where businesses set highly flexible prices for products or services based on the market demand at a particular time.

Now test yourself

9 Distinguish between a situation of excess production capacity and a lack of production capacity.
10 Briefly explain two methods of improving capacity utilisation.

Answers on p. 117

How to use technology to improve operational efficiency

Types of technology used in operations

Technology is changing quickly and affects how businesses produce goods and services as well as the products themselves. Technological developments that may affect production include:

- **More advanced computer systems**, for example enabling automated stock control systems and electronic data interchange.
- The **internet**, which enhances a business's ability to promote and sell products and its ability to communicate with customers.
- **Computer-aided manufacture (CAM)**, where manufacturers use robots as an integral part of the production process.
- **Computer-aided design (CAD)**, which can be linked to CAM systems.

Even small businesses can benefit from developments in stock control and design technology to improve the quality of their product or service. Such improvements will enable them to compete with larger-scale competitors.

The development of CAD has made the design of new products easier to carry out, store and alter. Modern software can also be used to estimate the cost of newly designed products. Technology has revolutionised manufacturing too. Computer-aided manufacturing is used by manufacturing firms of all sizes. Computers control the machines on the production line, saving labour and costs, and CAM systems can be linked to CAD technology to transform the entire process.

Benefits of new and updated technology

New technology offers businesses and consumers a range of benefits:
- It reduces unit costs of production, enhancing the competitiveness of the business concerned. For example, it allows publishers to send books electronically to be printed overseas, where costs are lower.
- For high-technology products, such as games consoles, it offers the opportunity to charge a premium price until the competition catches up. Such price skimming is likely to boost profits.
- A consistent standard of quality can be guaranteed through the use of CAM.
- Using technology efficiently may enable employees to work more efficiently. For example, electronic point of sale (EPOS) systems record information on sales and prices, and can be operated by the checkout operator in a shop as a routine part of work. EPOS automatically adjusts stock levels and reorders stock automatically as well as providing data to calculate sales revenue figures.
- It may allow access to new markets: for example, the internet allows potteries to sell worldwide.
- The use of technology can reduce waste, e.g. water control systems in commercial buildings recycle rainwater and other water for reuse within the business.

Costs of new and updated technology

New technology also poses difficulties for many businesses:
- It can be a drain on an organisation's capital. Firms may experience difficulty in raising the funds required to install high-technology equipment or to research a new product.
- It almost inevitably requires training of the existing workforce and perhaps recruitment of new employees. Both actions can create considerable costs for businesses.
- Its introduction may be met with opposition from existing employees, especially if job security is threatened. This may lead to industrial relations problems.

Now test yourself

TESTED ☐

11 Technology is a topic with links to many other areas of the specification. Divide a sheet of paper into four sections and label these as (i) marketing, (ii) finance, (iii) operations management and (iv) people in business. In each of the four sections compile a list of the implications for that function of the business of a decision to use new technology in producing a product or in the product itself.

Answer on p. 117

Making operational decisions to improve performance: improving quality

A quality product will satisfy customer needs and can be a major determinant of a business's competitiveness.

The importance of quality

Quality can be important to a business because it can:
- provide a USP, and give consumers a reason to buy the product
- allow a business to charge higher prices, increasing profit margins
- enable a business to increase its sales
- enhance reputation and brand loyalty

Methods of improving quality

When a business considers quality, it should not just be the end product or service that is considered: it should be the whole process of production from the acquisition of resources through to the final purchase and use of a product or service by the consumer. There are a number of ways this might be improved, as outlined below.

Quality assurance

Quality assurance refers to the mechanisms put in place to ensure that the entire operations process meets the required standards. With quality assurance it is the responsibility of all workers throughout the production process to make sure that each stage meets the required standard. As a result, employees have a greater responsibility and may become more engaged and motivated.

> **Quality assurance** is a system for ensuring the desired level of quality in the development, production and delivery of products or services.

Total quality management (TQM)

There are a number of different systems of quality assurance, of which **total quality management (TQM)** is probably the best known. TQM instils a culture of quality throughout the organisation. It places on all employees of a firm an individual and collective responsibility for maintaining high quality standards. By checking throughout the process, it aims for zero defects (see Figure 4.1).

> **Total quality management (TQM)** — where there is a culture of quality throughout the organisation.

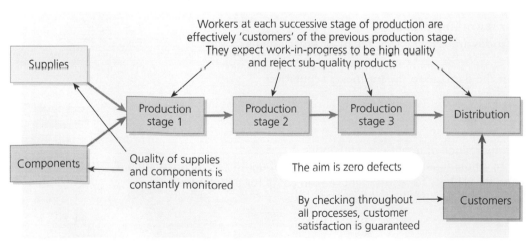

Figure 4.1 Total quality management

TQM has both an internal and an external dimension. Externally, the success of a firm depends on its ability to satisfy customers' demands. Product quality is likely to be a way in which a company can achieve a competitive advantage.

Internally, each department in a firm is viewed as a customer and/or a supplier. The firm has to meet consistently high standards in this 'internal' trading. Workers at each stage of the production process examine critically the work-in-progress they receive. Errors and faults are identified and rectified as soon as possible and customer satisfaction is assured.

Quality assurance systems are unlikely to succeed without the support of all employees. TQM seeks commitment to the highest quality standards in each of the internal stages of production. It minimises the time and money spent on quality by preventing quality problems.

Kaizen

Kaizen is the Japanese business philosophy of continuous improvement, where all employees are encouraged to identify and suggest possible improvements in the production process. Such a system requires a culture of participation and involvement.

The benefits and difficulties of improving quality

REVISED

The main **benefits** of improving quality are:
● an enhanced reputation and increased brand loyalty
● a competitive advantage in that quality may give a USP
● increased revenue due to higher sales and perhaps higher selling price
● greater flexibility in terms of price

The **difficulties** of improving quality might include:
● Bearing the cost of training of staff, the administration of the system and any equipment that might be needed.
● Employees can be resistant to change and convincing them that change is necessary might prove a stumbling block. Once convinced they might demand higher pay due to the increased responsibility.

The consequences of poor quality

REVISED

The consequences of poor quality revolve around the issue of increased costs including:
● the cost of scrapping or reworking products
● the additional costs if goods are returned for repair or replacement under warranty
● the costs resulting from the damage to the business's reputation

> **Exam tip**
>
> Implementing a system of TQM has enormous implications for the management of the workforce. It is likely to result in recruitment and training and can have a positive effect on motivation. Do seek to explore these links when responding to high-mark examination questions in this area.

> **Typical mistake**
>
> Only quality assurance is mentioned in the specification, and although some textbooks will cover quality control it is important the two are not confused.

> **Now test yourself**
>
> TESTED
>
> 12 Briefly explain the importance of quality to a business.
> 13 Explain one benefit to a business of introducing a system of quality assurance such as TQM.
> 14 Outline why poor quality is likely to result in increased costs for a business.
>
> Answers on p. 117

Making operational decisions to improve performance: managing inventory and supply chains

Inventory is the term used to describe stock. A business might hold stock in the form of raw materials and components, work in progress (products in the process of being made) and finished goods.

The **supply chain** encompasses three areas: the supply of materials to the manufacturer, the manufacturing process and the distribution of the finished goods to the consumer. In other words, the supply chain is the whole process of getting a good (or service) to the consumer.

> **Inventory** is the stock a business holds in the form of raw materials, components and work in progress.

Ways and value of improving flexibility, speed of response and dependability

REVISED

Whether it is a consumer buying the finished product or service or a business purchasing supplies, the dependability, speed of response and flexibility of the supplier are important factors that will affect the decision to buy. As a result, businesses will set operational objectives in this area.

Flexibility

Flexibility refers to the ability of a business to meet a customer's requirements whether in terms of numbers ordered or of variations in specification. The former refers to the ability to vary production levels in order to cope with variations in the size of order. The latter is known as **mass customisation** which means tailoring goods to specific customer requirements, e.g. in the car industry where an individual customer can effectively build his/her own car. The customer decides on the colour, paint, trim, seating material, accessories etc., this information is then sent to the factory and the car is produced. Greater flexibility is likely to lead to greater customer satisfaction and act as a competitive advantage.

> **Mass customisation** is the production of custom-tailored goods or services to meet customers' diverse and changing needs.

Speed of response and dependability

Speed of response refers to how quickly a business fulfils an order, and **dependability** refers to its punctuality or whether it fulfils the order on time. Responding in this way can result in a competitive advantage as this will lead to greater customer satisfaction and therefore loyalty. Such a response, however, relies on there being good communication and relationships with suppliers.

> **Typical mistake**
>
> The term 'dependability' can be used in two ways: for punctuality as outlined above, and also in terms of reliability and durability. It is important to identify the correct context when responding to a question.

How to manage supply to match demand and the value of doing so

REVISED

It is important that a business is able to match supply with demand. This is a particular problem for those businesses that operate in a seasonal industry, but it can also affect other businesses. Problems will arise if there are insufficient supplies to match demand and also if there is too much supply. Too little and a business will not only miss out on lucrative orders but also future orders due to lack of dependability. Too much supply will incur costs of holding the excess, and a business may be faced with selling the good at a reduced price. In order to overcome these problems, a business might either try to manage demand or manage the supply more effectively.

Managing demand

The marketing mix might be used in order to try to influence demand. It may be possible to increase demand by additional marketing, price reductions or sales promotions and, if necessary, decrease demand by reducing promotion and increasing price. Hotels and airlines are good examples of businesses that try to match supply and demand in this way. Center Parcs does this too, charging significantly higher prices in the school holidays and having more promotions during term times. As a result, it has a capacity utilisation of over 90%.

Managing supply

Supply can be managed in a number of ways:
- **Flexible workforce.** This can be achieved through the use of a multi-skilled workforce, employing part-time workers or workers on zero hours contracts. This enables a business to increase or decrease the amount produced by simply varying the size of the workforce or number of hours worked.
- **Increase capacity.** If the market a business is operating in is growing and further increases in demand are likely, it makes sense to invest in further capacity in order to be able to satisfy the growing demand.
- **Produce to order.** Some businesses, such as restaurants, tailors and aircraft manufacturers produce to order, but for others this is more difficult. As we have seen, however, the introduction of mass customisation has enabled more businesses to adopt this approach and, as technology develops further, more businesses are likely to be able to produce to order.
- **Outsourcing**. This is when another business is contracted to produce the extra goods required in order to satisfy the demand.

> **Outsourcing** is the transfer of production that was previously done in house to a third party.

Influences on the amount of inventory held

REVISED

Inventory as outlined above may be in the form of materials for production, work in progress and finished goods. It is important that a business holds sufficient inventory to be able to satisfy demand reliably. If it cannot do this it will run the risk of losing sales and damaging its reputation. The level of inventory held will depend on the following:
- **Nature of the product.** It would be foolish to hold large stocks of perishable goods.
- **Nature of production.** A JIT method of production means that lower levels of stock are held.
- **Nature of demand.** Seasonal products may require a higher level of stock to be held than those that have regular demand.
- **Opportunity cost.** Any money tied up in stock represents an opportunity cost and could be better used elsewhere in the business.

In order to manage inventory effectively a business might use an inventory control chart as shown in Figure 4.2.

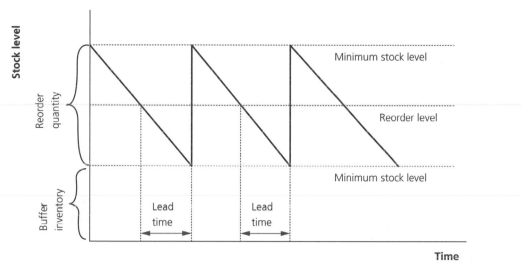

Figure 4.2 Inventory control chart

The key features of this chart are:
- **Buffer level of inventory:** the minimum amount of inventory held, designed to cover for emergencies such as late arrival of inventory.
- **Reorder level:** the level of inventory at which a new order is placed.
- **Lead time:** the time between an order being made and its arrival in the business.
- **Maximum stock level:** the highest amount of inventory a business is able to hold.
- **Reorder quantity:** the amount ordered.

Influences on the choice of suppliers

The choice of supplier may be influenced by a number of factors:
- **Dependability.** Is the supplier reliable and able to deliver on time?
- **Flexibility.** Is the supplier able to respond efficiently to changes in demand?
- **Quality.** Is the supplier able to produce at a consistent and reliable standard?
- **Price and payment terms.** Are the prices charged and payment terms (such as credit terms) competitive?
- **Ethics.** Does the supplier operate in a socially responsible manner? This might be of particular importance when dealing with overseas suppliers.

How to manage the supply chain effectively and efficiently and the value of this

A business will aim to have the right good in the right place at the right time. If it can achieve this effectively, it is likely to be able to gain customer loyalty and maximise revenues. This requires managers to make decisions about what to produce, when to produce and how much to produce. Getting this right requires not only good communication and relations with suppliers but also coordination with other functional areas — marketing, finance and human resources. It will also require an understanding of the external environment and how this might impact on both supply and demand.

TESTED

Now test yourself questions

15 Briefly outline how the nature of the product and the nature of demand might affect the level of inventory held.
16 Identify four key features of an inventory control chart.
17 In what circumstances might payment terms be more important than flexibility when choosing a supplier?

Answers on pp. 117–118

The value of outsourcing

REVISED

The value of outsourcing can be assessed by weighing up the benefits and drawbacks. One of the main benefits is that it enables a business to respond quicker to any increase in demand, thereby providing greater dependability for customers. It also means a business will save on costs as it will not have to invest in increasing capacity. This is particularly important if any increase in demand is only temporary.

Outsourcing does, however, have a number of drawbacks. One of the most important is the problem of quality: will the outsourced company be able to produce at the required level of quality? There is also the problem of cost: outsourcing is likely to be more costly than producing in house, and there may be other costs such as transport and distribution.

Outsourcing can work but it depends on the reliability and quality of work of the company undertaking the outsourced work and on the relationship established between the two companies.

Now test yourself

TESTED

18 Briefly explain the benefits of mass customisation.
19 How might a company offering skiing holidays use the marketing mix to manage demand?
20 Draw up a table to show the advantages and disadvantages of outsourcing.

Answers on p. 118

Exam practice

Alpha and Beta

Alpha and Beta are two businesses operating in the same market but with different approaches to production. Alpha has a very labour-intensive approach, whereas Beta is much more capital intensive as shown in the figures in the table below.

	Alpha	Beta
Output	500,000	450,000
Number of people employed	750	150
Turnover	£7m	£7.5m
Labour costs	£2m	£3.75m

In the face of increasing competition, particularly from overseas, over the last 10 years Beta has invested heavily in technology and adopted a lean production approach. It is now considering a further measure, that of just-in-time production. This, however, is considered to be a move too far by some of the directors, who believe that reliability and dependability has been a USP for their customers. A JIT approach could threaten this, particularly as they have had problems with their suppliers in the past. On these occasions it has been their sizeable buffer inventory that has enabled them to continue to meet customer deadlines.

Questions

a Sketch a simple Inventory control chart to illustrate buffer inventory. [4]

b For both Alpha and Beta, calculate the labour productivity and labour costs as a percentage of turnover. [6]

c Analyse the factors Beta may have considered before investing in technology. [9]

d To what extent do you believe some of the directors at Beta are right to be concerned about a move to just-in-time production? [16]

Answers and quick quiz 4 online

ONLINE

Summary

You should now have an understanding of all the points below.

Setting operational objectives

The value of setting and the internal and external influences on operational objectives

Analysing operational performance

- interpretation of operational data including calculation of labour productivity, unit costs, capacity and capacity utilisation
- the use of data in operational decision-making

Making operational decisions to improve performance: increasing efficiency and productivity

- capacity and its efficient utilisation
- the importance of labour productivity, how to increase it and difficulties involved
- choosing the optimal use of resources
- lean production including JIT
- using technology to improve operational efficiency

Making operational decisions to improve performance: improving quality

- the importance of quality and the consequences of poor quality
- methods of improving quality (including quality assurance) and benefits and difficulties of doing so

Making operational decisions to improve performance: managing inventory and supply chains

- ways and value of improving flexibility, speed of response and dependability
- the value of managing supply to match demand including outsourcing, producing to order and flexible workforce
- influences on the amount of inventory held including interpreting inventory control charts
- influences on the choice of suppliers

5 Decision-making to improve financial performance

Setting financial objectives

When judging the performance of a business, most analysts will first look at the financial information. It is therefore very important that a business sets objectives in terms of revenue, costs, profit, return on capital, cash flow and capital structure.

The value of setting financial objectives

REVISED

There are a number of benefits of setting financial objectives:
- They may act as a measure of performance.
- They provide targets which can be a focus for decision-making.
- Potential investors or creditors may be able to assess the viability of the business.

The distinction between cash flow and profit

REVISED

Cash flow and profit are very different. **Cash flow** is the difference between the actual amount of money a business receives (inflows) and the actual amount it pays out (outflows), whereas **profit** is the difference between all sales revenue (even if payment has not yet been received) and expenditure. It is possible for a profitable business to have cash-flow problems. In fact, many small businesses fail not because they are not profitable but because they have cash-flow problems. Such problems can occur for a number of reasons including:
- holding large amounts of inventory (stock)
- having sales on long credit periods
- using cash to purchase fixed assets

This distinction between cash flow and profit highlights the importance to a business of setting clear cash-flow objectives.

> ### Now test yourself
>
> TESTED
>
> 1 How is it possible that a seemingly profitable business can fail?
>
> **Answer on p. 118**

The distinction between gross profit, operating profit and profit for the year

REVISED

When looking at profit it is important to distinguish between three aspects:
- **Gross profit.** This is the difference between a business's sales revenue and the direct costs of production such as materials and direct labour. It is calculated in the following way:

sales revenue – direct costs of production = gross profit

- **Operating profit (profit of operations).** This is the difference between the gross profit and the indirect costs of production or expenses such as marketing and salaries. In other words, it is sales revenue minus both direct and indirect costs of production. It may be calculated in the following ways:

sales revenue – all costs of production = operating profit

gross profit – expenses = operating profit

- **Profit for the year.** The figure for operating profit does not include other expenditure such as interest payments or tax to be paid or other income such as interest received or money received from the sale of assets. It can be calculated in the following way:

operating profit + other income – other expenditure = profit for the year

Now test yourself

TESTED

2 Distinguish between the following three measures of profit: gross profit; operating profit and profit for the year.

Answer on p. 118

Revenue, costs and profit objectives

REVISED

A business is likely to set targets in terms of **revenue**, **costs** and **profit**.

Revenue

A knowledge of the likely revenue of a business is essential and is the starting-point for creating a budget. Budgeted revenue might be based on the objective of increasing revenue by 5% per annum. The objective set might depend on the type of market a business is operating in and the state of the economy. In addition, any objective set would have to be coordinated with the other functional areas such as marketing and operations.

Cost

Businesses operate in a highly competitive environment and, as a result, face increasing pressure on costs. Cost minimisation, therefore, has become an important business objective. This involves trying to achieve the lowest possible unit costs of production. As an alternative to cost minimisation, a business might set an objective of reducing costs by a certain percentage or target a specific area of the business that is seen to be underperforming.

Profit

Making a profit is the aim of the majority of businesses in the private sector. A business might, however, set a specific objective for profit. This might be a particular figure, a percentage increase, or it might be set in terms of a profit margin. Profit maximisation is sometimes mentioned, but it is difficult to judge whether profit maximisation has actually been achieved, and a business making unreasonably high profit can be the subject of a great deal of criticism as in the case with some of the utility companies.

Cash-flow objectives

REVISED

Cash flow is the flow of money into and out of the business and is vital to the health of any business. Although it is possible to survive as a business in the short to medium term whilst making a loss, it is impossible to survive for long without cash to make immediate payments. It is therefore vital that a business manages its cash flow carefully. This may involve setting cash–flow objectives such as:

- targets for monthly closing balances
- reduction of bank borrowings to a target level
- reduction of seasonality in sales
- targets for achieving payment from customers
- extension of the business's credit period to pay suppliers

These objectives are likely to vary according to the circumstances of the individual business.

> **Cash flow** is the money (cash) moving into and out of a business over a given period of time.

Objectives for investment (capital expenditure) levels

REVISED

Capital expenditure is the money spent on fixed assets such as buildings and equipment and represents long-term investment into the business. Such investment will take place when a business first sets up, but it will also need to invest further as a business grows and develops. Objectives for investment will depend on the overall corporate objectives. For example, if there is an overall objective of growth, this is likely to require further capital expenditure. It will also depend on other factors such as the type of business and the state of the economy and market in which the business is operating. For example, with oil prices falling, many oil companies, such as BP and Shell, are cutting back investment in exploration.

> **Capital expenditure** is the money used to purchase, upgrade or improve the life of long-term assets.

Return on investment

A business might set itself an objective in terms of the return on an investment, e.g. 10%. This would be calculated using the following formula:

$$\frac{\text{return on investment (or profit)}}{\text{capital invested}} \times 100$$

This formula could also be used when a business is deciding between two different investments. With this type of decision, however, it is important to remember that any returns (profit) will only be forecasts, and any predictions made may be influenced by a manager's own bias towards a particular investment.

Capital structure objectives

REVISED

The capital structure of the business refers to the long-term capital (finance) of a business. Long-term capital is made up of **equity** (share capital) and **borrowing** (loan capital). The proportion of borrowing to equity is an important consideration for a business. The higher the borrowing, the greater is the interest repayment. Having high interest payments could put a business at risk if profit should fall for any reason. In addition, any rise in interest rates could have a significant impact on

> **Equity** is the money a business raises through the issue of shares.
>
> **Borrowing** is the money a business raises through loan capital.

profit. A business may therefore set targets in terms of the proportion of long-term capital that is debt. This can be measured by the following gearing ratio:

$$\text{gearing ratio} = \frac{\text{loan capital}}{\text{total capital}} \times 100$$

total capital = loan capital + equity

Now test yourself

3 What is the formula used for calculating return on investment?

4 Briefly explain how a highly geared business selling luxury items might be affected by a rise in interest rates.

Answers on p. 118

External and internal influences on financial objectives and decisions

External influences

- **Competitor actions.** Businesses operate within a competitive environment and therefore financial objectives may be affected by the actions of competitors. This might be due to competitors launching a new marketing campaign, price cuts or the development of new products or services.
- **Market forces.** Markets and fashion change over time and, unless a business can lead or keep up with changes, financial targets may be missed. This can be illustrated by the changes in the music and film industry where HMV and Blockbuster failed to recognise the growth in downloading.
- **Economic factors.** Changes in the economy, such as the recession of 2008, are likely to result in financial targets being missed, whereas increasing growth may lead to better performance. Changes in interest rates can also impact on performance illustrating the need for all businesses to review targets in the light of any changes in the economy.
- **Political factors.** Change of government and legislation can also have an impact. For instance, an increase in the minimum wage or the introduction of new health and safety legislation will incur additional costs which, if not passed on to the consumer, will impact on financial targets.
- **Technology.** Changes in technology may impact in a number of ways such as facilitating quicker and easier monitoring of financial data. The introduction of new technology, which may, in the long term, lead to greater efficiency and improved performance, is likely to have a significant cost in the short term.

Internal influences

- **Corporate objectives.** Any financial targets need to be linked to the overall corporate objectives. For instance, an objective of growth might lead to improved financial performance in the long term, but in the short term to a decline in performance as more money is used to finance growth.

- **Resources available.** The ability to achieve financial targets may be limited by the resources available, such as the availability of skilled labour and the money available to finance the targets set.
- **Operational factors.** The ability to achieve financial targets will be limited in the short term by the physical capacity of a business.

Now test yourself

TESTED

5 Why might a business not be able to achieve its financial targets even though market conditions are favourable?

Answer on p. 118

Analysing financial performance

How to construct and analyse budgets and cash-flow forecasts

REVISED

A **budget** is a financial plan. Its purpose is to provide a target for entrepreneurs and managers as well as a basis for a later assessment of the performance of a business. A budget should have a specific purpose and must have a set of targets attached to it if it is to be of value. The detail of a budget should be the result of negotiation with all concerned. If it is to work as an effective motivator, those responsible for keeping to a budget should play a part in setting it.

> A **budget** is a financial plan.

Structure of income, expenditure and profit budgets

Income budgets

Income budgets are forecasted earnings from sales and are sometimes called 'sales budgets'. For a newly established business they will be based on the results of market research. Established businesses can also call upon past trading records to provide information for sales forecasts. Income budgets are normally drawn up for the next financial year, on a monthly basis, as shown in Table 5.1.

> An **income budget** is the forecasted earnings from sales, sometimes called a 'sales budget'.

Expenditure budgets

An **expenditure budget** sets out the expected spending of a business, broken down into a number of categories. The titles given to these categories will depend upon the type of business. A manufacturing business will have sections entitled 'Raw materials' or 'Components', whereas a service business may not. The categories in Table 5.1 may therefore vary according to the type of business.

> An **expenditure budget** is the expected spending of a business.

Profit (or loss) budgets

Profit and loss budgets are calculated by subtracting forecast expenditure (or costs) from forecast sales income. Depending on the balance between expenditure and income, a loss or a profit may be forecast. It is not unusual for a new business to forecast (and actually make) a loss during its first period of trading.

Table 5.1 shows forecast income, expenditure and profit/loss for a newly established manufacturer of surfboards for the first 3 months of trading.

Table 5.1 Viking Boards Ltd's budget (April to June)

	April (£)	May (£)	June (£)
Cash sales	10,215	15,960	17,500
Credit sales	0	0	4,125
Total sales	**10,215**	**15,960**	**21,625**
Purchases of raw materials and components	19,500	14,010	15,550
Interest payments	1,215	1,105	1,350
Wages and salaries	3,000	2,850	2,995
Marketing and administration	2,450	2,400	2,450
Other costs	975	1,100	1,075
Total costs	**27,140**	**21,465**	**23,420**
Profit/(loss)	**(16,925)**	**(5,505)**	**(1,795)**

The process of setting budgets

As Table 5.1 shows, budgets have a common structure. The top of the budget shows income, and this is followed by expenditure and finally by profit or loss. This is also the sequence in which budgets are set. Figure 5.1 summarises this process.

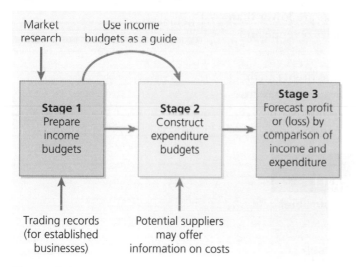

Figure 5.1 The process of setting budgets

Businesses set budgets because:

- They are an essential element of a business plan. A bank is unlikely to grant a loan without evidence of this particular form of financial planning.
- Budgets can help businesses to decide whether or not to go ahead with a business idea. If the budget shows a significant loss in its first year of trading, with little improvement evident, then the business idea may be abandoned.
- Budgets can help with pricing decisions. If a large loss is forecast, the business may decide to adjust the price to improve the business's financial prospects.

Difficulties of setting budgets

Those in charge of budgets can expect to face several difficulties when drawing up a first set of budgets:

- In some cases there may be no historical evidence available to a business, particularly for a new business or an existing business entering a new market. There will be no trading records to show the level of sales income, costs or how these figures fluctuated throughout the year.
- Forecasting costs can also be problematic. A business may lack the experience to estimate costs such as those for raw materials or wages.
- Competitors may respond to the actions of a business by cutting prices or promoting their products heavily. This can affect the sales income of a business and it may receive less income than it forecast. As a result, expenditure on promotion may have to increase, so increasing costs.

How to calculate and interpret variances

Variance analysis is the study by managers of the differences between planned activities in the form of budgets and the actual results that were achieved. Table 5.2 is an example of a monthly budget for a restaurant.

As the period covered by the budget unfolds, actual results can be compared with the budgeted figures and variances calculated and examined.

A **positive (or favourable) variance** occurs when costs are lower than forecast or profit or revenues higher, as in the case of sales revenue and profits in Table 5.2.

A **negative (or adverse) variance** arises when costs are higher than expected or revenues are less than anticipated. Examples are wages costs and food and drink in Table 5.2.

Variance analysis is the study by managers of the differences between planned activities in the form of budgets and the actual results that were achieved.

Table 5.2 An example of calculating variances

Item	Budget figure (£)	Actual figure (£)	Variance (£)
Sales revenue	39,500	42,420	2,920 (favourable)
Fixed costs	9,500	9,500	0
Wages costs	10,450	11,005	555 (adverse)
Food and drink	8,475	9,826	1,351 (adverse)
Other costs	5,300	6,000	700 (adverse)
Total costs	33,725	36,331	2,606 (adverse)
Profit/loss	5,775	6,089	314 (favourable)

How to use variances to inform decision-making

Positive variances might occur because of good budgetary control or by accident, e.g. due to rising market prices. Possible responses to positive variances are:

- to increase production if prices are rising, giving increased profit margins
- to reduce prices if costs are below expectations and the business aims to increase its sales
- to reinvest into the business or pay shareholders higher dividends if profits exceed expectations

Negative variances might occur because of inadequate control or factors outside the firm's control, such as rising raw material costs. Possible responses to negative variances are:

- to reduce costs (e.g. by buying less expensive materials)
- to increase advertising in order to increase sales of the product and revenues
- to reduce prices to increase sales (relies on demand being price elastic)

The key issue about using the results of variance analysis to help decision-making is to take into account the causes of the adverse or favourable variances. Just because a result is favourable does not mean that everything is in order. Neither does an adverse variance mean that the area responsible has been inefficient. A favourable production material variance could be generated from using lower-quality raw materials, which in turn could manifest itself as a drop in sales. Similarly, an adverse cost variance may occur because sales are higher than forecast and the business has incurred extra costs in supplying customers' demands.

The value of budgeting

REVISED

The value of budgeting can be assessed by weighing up the benefits and drawbacks of using budgets.

Benefits of budgets

- Targets can be set for each part of a business, allowing managers to identify the extent to which each part contributes to the business's performance.
- Inefficiency and waste can be identified, so that appropriate remedial action can be taken.
- Budgets make managers think about the financial implications of their actions and focus decision-making on the achievement of objectives.
- Budgeting should improve financial control by preventing overspending.
- Budgets can help improve internal communication.
- Delegated or devolved budgets can be used as a motivator by giving employees authority and the opportunity to fulfil some of their higher-level needs, as identified by Maslow (see pp. 106–107). At the same time, senior managers can retain control of the business by monitoring budgets.

> **Typical mistake**
>
> When answering questions on the value of budgets students often write only about the use of budgets in preventing overspending. Make sure that you can argue a wider range of points.

Drawbacks of budgets

- The operation of budgets can become inflexible. For example, sales may be lost if the marketing budget is followed when competitors implement major promotional campaigns.
- Budgets have to be accurate to have any meaning. Wide variances between budgeted and actual figures can demotivate staff and waste the resources used to prepare the budgets.

> **Exam tip**
>
> Look for the relationships between revenues, costs and profits when considering variances. For example, if sales revenue has recorded a negative variance, it would be reasonable to expect costs, especially variable costs, to show a positive variance. If they do not, profits are likely to have a negative variance.

Now test yourself

6 Draw up a table to show four possible causes of favourable variances and four possible causes of adverse variances. For each cause of variance that you have listed, identify an appropriate response.
7 Briefly outline three benefits of budgeting.

Answer on p. 118

The structure of a cash-flow forecast

Cash-flow forecasts are a central part of a business plan for a new business. They comprise three sections:

- **Receipts** in which the expected total month-by-month receipts are recorded.
- **Payments** in which the expected monthly expenditure by item is recorded.
- **Running balance** in which a running total of the expected bank balance at the beginning and end of each month (see Figure 5.1) is recorded. These are termed 'opening' and 'closing balances'. The closing balance at the end of one month becomes the opening balance at the start of the next month.

Negative figures in cash-flow forecasts are usually shown in brackets.

Month	Jan	Feb	Mar	Apr	May	June
Receipts						
1 Sales cash	4,500					
2 Sales credit	3,650					
3 Total cash in (1 + 2)	8,150					
Payments						
4 Supplies	2,500					
5 Wages	1,900					
6 Fuel	900					
7 Electricity	200					
8 Heating	200					
9 Rates	400					
10 Mortgage payment	900					
11 Interest on loan	450					
12 Total cash out (4 + 5 + 6... + 11)	7,450					
13 Net cash flow (3 − 12)	700					
14 Opening bank balance	(250)	450				
15 Closing bank balance (14 + 13)	450					

Figure 5.2 An example of a cash-flow forecast completed for the month of January

> **Typical mistake**
>
> It is not unusual for a cash-flow calculation in an examination to include negative figures. Many students have difficulty carrying out calculations involving negative figures and make errors when adding and subtracting where one or more figure is negative.

How to construct and interpret breakeven charts

A breakeven chart is a graph used in breakeven analysis to illustrate the point at which total costs are equal to total revenue, in other words, the output at which it makes neither a profit nor a loss.

How to construct a breakeven chart

One way of representing the breakeven point is through the use of a breakeven chart, as shown in Figure 5.3. The step-by-step points below show how to draw a breakeven chart.

1 Give the chart a title.
2 Label axes (horizontal — output in units; vertical — costs/revenues in pounds).
3 Draw on the fixed cost line.
4 Draw on the variable cost line.
5 Draw on the total cost line.
6 Draw on the sales revenue line.
7 Label the breakeven point where sales revenue = total cost.
8 Mark on the selected operating point (SOP): that is, the actual or forecast level of the company's output.
9 Mark on the margin of safety (the difference between the SOP and the breakeven level of output).
10 Mark clearly the amount of profit and loss. Note that this is a vertical distance at any given level of production, and not an area.

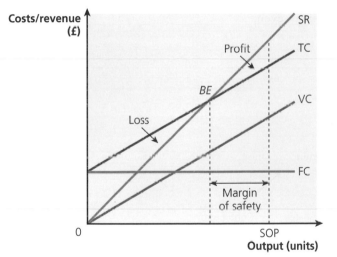

Figure 5.3 A breakeven chart for product X

> **Exam tip**
>
> It is unlikely that you will be asked to draw a complete breakeven chart in an examination as this would take too long. It is probable that you will be asked to add lines to an incomplete chart or to show the effects of changes in costs or prices. You should practise these types of activity.

Contribution and the calculation of breakeven output

The breakeven output can also be identified through calculation, and doing so enables the accuracy of charts to be checked. An understanding of the concept of **contribution** is necessary for this. Contribution is the difference between sales revenue and variable costs and can be calculated as follows:

> **sales revenue – variable costs**

> **Contribution** is the amount of money left over after variable costs have been subtracted from sales revenue.

It can also be calculated per unit as follows:

> **sales price per unit – variable cost per unit**

From this second calculation you may have already spotted that total contribution could also be calculated by multiplying unit contribution with output:

> **total contribution = unit contribution × output**

Contribution can be used to calculate two things:
● the breakeven point
● the level of profit

The calculation for breakeven is:

> $$\frac{\textbf{fixed costs}}{\textbf{contribution per unit}}$$

This tells us the number of units that need to be sold to break even.

Profit can be calculated as follows:

> **contribution total – fixed costs**

Figure 5.4 illustrates how the profit calculation works.

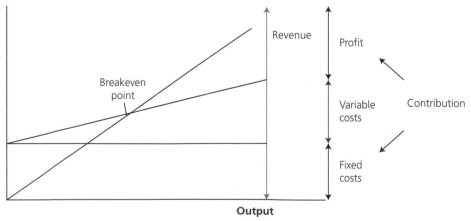

Figure 5.4 Profit calculation

From Figure 5.4 it can be seen that contribution is made up of profit and fixed costs. Therefore, by subtracting the fixed costs we are left with profit. Note also that at the breakeven point no profit is made, so the value of contribution must be equal to the value of fixed costs. This means that below the breakeven point any contribution sales goes towards covering the fixed cost, and above the breakeven point it goes towards profit.

Now test yourself

8 What is the formula used to calculate breakeven?
9 A business sells 100,000 burgers per year for an average price of £2.50. The average variable cost for each burger is £1.50. Calculate the total contribution for the year.
10 A business produces 10,000 units. It has a sales price of £5 per unit, variable costs of £3 per unit and fixed costs of £15,000. Calculate (i) the breakeven output and (ii) the level of profit made.

Answers on p. 118

How to calculate and illustrate on a breakeven chart the effects of changes in price, output and cost

Breakeven analysis can illustrate the effects of changes in price and costs, and assist entrepreneurs in making decisions by the use of 'what if?' scenarios:

- What level of output and sales will be needed to break even if we sell at a price of £x per unit?
- What would be the effect on the level of output and sales needed to break even of an x% rise (or fall) in fixed or variable costs?

Using breakeven analysis in this way, entrepreneurs can decide whether it is likely to be profitable to supply a product at a certain price or to start production. This aspect of breakeven analysis makes it a valuable technique. Few businesses trade in environments in which changes in prices and costs do not occur regularly.

Figure 5.5 illustrates the effects of changes in key variables on the breakeven chart. These are further illustrated in Table 5.3.

Typical mistake

When adding or amending lines on breakeven charts do not waste time by plotting figures at each level of output before drawing the new line. All lines on breakeven charts are straight, so it is only necessary to plot the new figures at zero and maximum output and to join up these two points using a ruler.

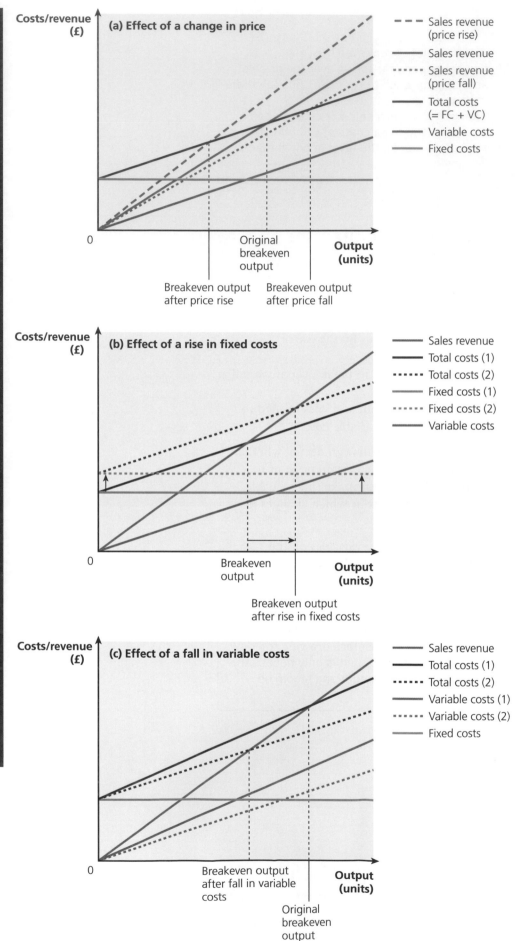

Figure 5.5 Effects of changes in key variables on the breakeven chart

Note: Figure 5.5(b) only illustrates a rise in fixed costs to avoid the diagram becoming too complex. A fall in fixed costs would have the exact opposite effect. For the same reason, Figure 5.5(c) only illustrates a fall in variable costs. A rise in variable costs would have the exact opposite effect.

Table 5.3 Effects of changes in key variables on the breakeven chart

Change in key variable	Impact on breakeven chart	Effect on breakeven output	Explanation of change	Illustrated in figure
Increase in selling price.	Revenue line pivots upwards.	Breakeven is reached at a lower level of output.	Fewer sales will be necessary to break even because each sale generates more revenue, while costs have not altered.	Figure 5.5(a)
Fall in selling price.	Revenue line pivots downwards.	A higher level of output is necessary to reach breakeven.	Each sale will earn less revenue for the business and, because costs have not altered, more sales will be required to break even.	Figure 5.5(a)
Rise in fixed costs.	Parallel upward shift in fixed and total cost lines.	Breakeven occurs at a higher level of output.	More sales will be required to break even because the business has to pay higher costs before even starting production.	Figure 5.5(b)
Fall in fixed costs.	Parallel downward shift in fixed and total cost lines.	Smaller output required to break even.	Because the business faces lower costs, fewer sales will be needed to ensure that revenue matches costs.	
Rise in variable costs.	Total cost line pivots upwards.	Higher output needed to break even.	Each unit of output costs more to produce, so a greater number of sales will be necessary if the firm is to break even.	
Fall in variable costs.	Total cost line pivots downwards.	Lower level of output needed to break even.	Every unit of production is produced more cheaply, so less output and fewer sales are necessary to break even.	Figure 5.5(c)

The value of breakeven analysis

REVISED

The value of breakeven analysis can be assessed by weighing up the benefits and shortcomings.

Benefits include:
- **Starting a new business.** A business can estimate the level of sales required before it would start to make a profit. From this it can see whether or not the business proposal is viable. The results of market research are important here.
- **Supporting loan applications.** A business will be unlikely to succeed in negotiating a loan with a bank unless it has carried out a range of financial planning, including breakeven analysis.
- **Measuring profit and losses.** In diagrammatic form, breakeven analysis enables businesses to tell at a glance what their estimated level of profit or loss would be at any level of output and sales.

- **Modelling 'what if?' scenarios.** Breakeven analysis enables businesses to model what will happen to their level of profit if they change prices or are faced by changes in costs.

Although breakeven analysis is quick to perform, it is a simplification and as such it has several **drawbacks**:

- No costs are truly fixed. A stepped fixed cost line would be a better representation, as fixed costs are likely to increase in the long term and at higher levels of output if more production capacity is required.
- The total cost line should not be represented by a straight line because this takes no account of the discounts available for bulk buying.
- Sales revenue assumes that all output produced is sold and at a uniform price, which is unrealistic.
- The analysis is only as good as the information provided. Collecting accurate information is expensive, and in many cases the cost of collection would outweigh any benefit that breakeven analysis could provide.

> **Exam tip**
>
> It is common for examination questions to ask you to read data from breakeven charts. You may be required to read off profit or loss, revenue or variable costs. You should practise doing this.

Now test yourself

TESTED

11 What will be the effect on breakeven output of (i) a rise in fixed costs and (ii) an increase in price?
12 Explain two weaknesses of using breakeven analysis as a technique of financial planning.

Answers on p. 118

How to analyse profitability

REVISED

The figures for gross profit, operating profit and profit for the year can be used to analyse the performance of a business in terms of its profitability. On their own, however, they show very little and, in order to be useful, they need to be compared either with previous years or other companies. The most useful way of doing this is to convert them into ratios and calculate the percentage profit margins. This can be done as follows:

$$\text{gross profit margin} = \frac{\text{gross profit}}{\text{sales revenue}} \times 100$$

$$\text{operating profit margin} = \frac{\text{operating profit}}{\text{sales revenue}} \times 100$$

$$\text{profit for the year margin} = \frac{\text{profit for the year}}{\text{sales revenue}} \times 100$$

Once calculated, these figures make comparisons both with previous years and other firms simpler and easier to understand. For example, when comparing different supermarket chains, their levels of turnover and profit will be different. By calculating operating profit margins it will be possible to see at a glance what percentage of every pound of turnover is profit — the higher the figure the better. In addition, the gross and operating profit margins give an indication of a business's ability to control both its direct and indirect costs. A falling gross profit margin could indicate either rising direct costs of production or a more competitive environment and falling prices. A falling operating profit margin could indicate rising indirect costs (expenses).

> **Exam tip**
>
> When assessing the performance of a business try to make comparisons either with previous years' figures or the performance of other similar businesses.

Now test yourself

13 Briefly explain how it might be possible for a business to have an improving gross profit margin but a falling operating profit margin.

Answer on p. 118

How to analyse the timings of cash inflows and outflows

Money leaving a business is known as **payables**, and money coming into the business is known as **receivables**. The analysis of this relationship is important as it will enable a business to:

- Forecast periods of time when cash outflows might exceed cash inflows and take action (e.g. arrange a loan) in order to avoid the business being unable to pay bills on time.
- Plan when and how to finance major items of expenditure (e.g. vehicles or machinery), which may lead to large outflows of cash.
- Highlight any periods when cash surpluses, that could be used elsewhere, may exist.
- Assess whether an idea will generate enough cash to be worthwhile putting into action.
- Give evidence to lenders (e.g. banks) that any loans given can and will be repaid.

> **Payables** (sometimes called 'trade creditors') — money owed for goods and services that have been purchased on credit.
>
> **Receivables** (sometimes called 'trade debtors') — money owed by a business's customers for goods or services purchased on credit.

Now test yourself

14 Distinguish between payables and receivables.
15 Why is it important that a business draws up a cash-flow forecast? Identify three reasons.

Answers on p. 119

The use of data for financial decision-making and planning

A business today has enormous amounts of data at its disposal, which can be manipulated in a variety of ways. This involves employing a scientific decision-making approach using budgets, cash flows, breakeven and profit ratios, which will hopefully reduce risk. Any data used, however, will either be historical or forecast and should be treated with a certain amount of caution.

Making financial decisions: sources of finance

Internal and external sources of finance

Figure 5.6 summarises the various sources of finance available to a business.

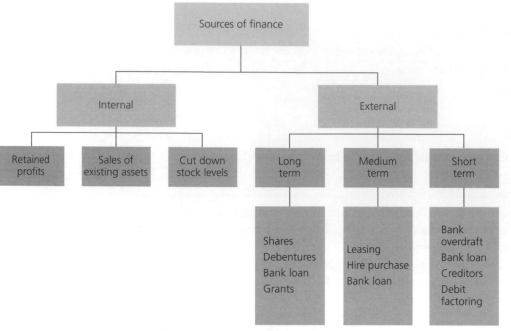

Figure 5.6 Sources of finance

External

The two main external sources of long-term capital, **equity** and **loans**, were outlined when discussing the capital structure of a business above (see p. 74).

- **Equity** is the money provided by the owners or shareholders. Its key characteristics are that it will not have to be paid back and there is no interest to pay on it. If a shareholder wishes to regain his/her money, he/she will simply sell his/her shares to someone else through the Stock Exchange. Although the owners of the shares receive no interest payment, they will be hopeful of receiving a share of the profit made through a dividend payment.
- **Loans** is money raised from a creditor, but unlike equity loans have to be paid back and there will also be interest payments to be made.

Other sources of long-term external finance include:

- **Venture capital.** This applies to mainly small and medium-sized businesses that may struggle to raise money from traditional sources. A venture capitalist may provide funds as a loan or in return for a share of the business.
- **Mortgages.** A loan granted for the purpose of buying land or buildings.
- **Crowdfunding.** This is a method of raising finance from a large number of people who each contribute a small amount of money. This has been made possible through the internet, an example being Lunar Missions Ltd, a private moon drilling mission that has raised over $1m by this method.

Internal

There are two major sources of internal finance: **retained profit** and **sale of assets**.

- **Retained profit.** This is profit that is not paid to shareholders and is kept within the business for future investment. A business will only have access to this source if it is profit-making, but the great benefit is that it does not have to be paid back and has no interest or dividend payment attached to it.

- **Sale of assets.** This is when a business sells assets it no longer requires, such as machinery, warehouse and factory space or land. Although this can sometimes raise large amounts, a business has to be sure that these assets will not be required in the future.

Short-term sources of finance

Short-term sources of finance include the following:
- **Overdraft.** This is when a bank allows a business to overspend on its bank account up to an agreed limit. Overdrafts are easy to arrange and are a very flexible form of finance. They can be expensive, but interest will only be charged on the amount overdrawn.
- **Debt factoring.** This is when a business sells its bills (invoices) that have not been paid to a bank or financial institution in order to access this money up front. The business receives 80% of the sum owed immediately and the remainder less any charges once the bank or finance institution has collected the money.
- **Trade credit.** This is when a business receives materials but pays for them at a later date. Trade credit periods can vary from a week to several months.

Advantages and disadvantages of different sources of finance for short- and long-term uses

REVISED

Table 5.5

Source	Advantages	Disadvantages
Retained profit	• No interest to pay. • Does not have to be paid back. • No dilution of shares.	• Shareholders may have reduced dividends.
Sale of assets	• No interest to pay. • Does not have to be paid back. • No dilution of shares.	• Once sold gone forever.
Equity	• No interest to pay. • Does not have to be paid back.	• Might upset existing shareholders.
Loans	• No dilution of shares.	• Interest payments. • Set maturity date.
Overdraft	• Quick and easy to set up and very flexible. • Interest paid only on amount overdrawn.	• Interest payments higher than for a loan.
Debt factoring	• Immediate cash. • Improves cash flow. • Protection from bad debts. Reduced administration costs.	• Expensive. • Customer relations may be affected.
Trade credit	• Eases cash flow.	• If late paying, can damage credit history.

Now test yourself

TESTED

16 How does an overdraft differ from a bank loan?

17 Explain why retained profit and equity might be viewed as preferable sources of finance to borrowing.

Answers on p. 119

Making financial decisions: improving cash flow and profits

Cash-flow problems

Cash-flow problems may occur for a number of reasons:

- **Poor management.** If managers do not forecast and monitor the business's cash flow, problems are more likely to arise and lead to a serious financial situation. Similarly, the failure to chase up customers who have not paid can lead to lower inflows and cash shortages.
- **Giving too much trade credit.** When a firm offers trade credit, it gives its customers time to settle their accounts — possibly 30, 60 or 90 days. This is an interest-free loan, and while it may attract customers it slows the business's cash inflows, reducing its cash balance.
- **Overtrading.** This occurs when a business expands rapidly without planning how to finance the expansion. A growing business must pay for materials and labour before receiving the cash inflow from sales. If it does this on an increasing scale it may struggle to fund its expenditure.
- **Unexpected expenditure.** A business may incur unexpected costs, resulting in a cash outflow. The breakdown of a machine can lead to significant outflows of cash, weakening the enterprise's cash position.

Methods of improving cash flow

There are a number of methods of improving cash flow.

Factoring

Factoring enables a business to sell its outstanding debtors to a specialist debt collector, called a factor. The business receives about 80% of the value of the debt immediately. The factor then receives payment from the customer and passes on the balance to the firm, holding back about 5% to cover expenses. This improves the business's cash-flow position as it does not have to wait for payment. Factoring, however, reduces profit margins, as approximately 5% of revenue is 'lost'.

Sale and leaseback

Here the owner of an asset (such as property) sells it and then leases it back. This provides a short-term boost to the business's finances, as the sale of the asset generates revenue. However, the business commits itself to paying rent to use the asset for the foreseeable future.

Improved working capital control

Working capital is the cash available to a business for its day-to-day operations. This can help cash-flow management and be improved by:

- selling stocks of finished goods quickly, prompting cash inflows
- making customers pay on time and offering less trade credit (although this may damage sales)
- persuading suppliers to offer longer periods of trade credit, slowing cash outflows

Other possibilities are:

- stimulating sales, by offering discounts for cash and prompt payment
- selling off excess material stocks

> **Working capital** is the cash available to a business for its day-to-day operations.

18 Draw up a two-column table to show four possible causes of cash-flow problems. In each case suggest an appropriate solution.

Answer on p. 119

Methods of improving profits and profitability

 REVISED

Profitability measures profits against some yardstick, such as the sales revenue achieved by the business. Firms can increase their profits and/or profitability by taking a variety of actions:

- **Increasing prices.** An increase in price may increase revenue without raising total costs. However, this is a risk because an increase in price may cause a fall in sales, leading to a reduction in profits if the fall in sales more than offsets the increase in price. The extent to which this happens depends upon price elasticity of demand (see pp. 38–39).
- **Cutting costs.** Lower costs of production can increase profit margins but possibly at the expense of quality. Reduced quality could reduce the volume of sales and the firm's reputation.
- **Using its capacity as fully as possible.** If a business has productive capacity that is not being utilised, its profits will be lower than they could be. If train companies run services that are only 50% occupied, their revenue is much lower. Offering incentives to customers to use the trains could increase profits, as it costs little more to run a full train than a half-full one.
- **Increasing efficiency.** Avoiding waste in the form of poor quality and unsaleable products, using staff fully and using minimal resources to make products are all ways of improving the efficiency of a business. Improving efficiency is likely to result in increased profits.

> **Profitability** measures profits against some yardstick, such as the sales revenue achieved by the business.

Difficulties of improving cash flow and profit

REVISED

It is relatively easy in theory to identify ways of improving cash flow and profit but much more difficult in practice. This is due to the difficulties associated with each method. The relative difficulties are summarised below.

Cash flow

- **Factoring.** The profit margin is reduced due to cost of factoring. In addition, customers might become concerned that their supplier has cash-flow difficulties.
- **Sale and lease back.** The asset is removed forever and rent now has to be paid.
- **Working capital control.** Customers may be put off by reduced credit periods and suppliers may be unwilling to extend credit periods.

Profit

- **Increasing prices.** This may reduce sales and revenue and attract criticism from customers.
- **Cutting costs.** This is likely to result in a reduction in quality if inferior raw materials are used. It could also mean job losses and upset labour relations.
- **Use capacity fully.** This may cause problems in matching supply with demand. It could result in price reductions and lower revenues.
- **Increasing efficiency.** This may result in redundancies if technology is introduced.

Now test yourself

19 Identify two ways in which a business could increase its profit.
20 For each of the methods of increasing profit, outline the difficulties that might be encountered.

Answers on p. 119

Exam practice

Opportunity knocks for ABC plc

ABC currently operates on two separate sites, which although workable does mean higher costs than necessary. The opportunity has arisen to purchase land adjacent to one of the sites and consolidate production into one area. This would have a significant impact on costs, especially fixed costs, and as a result lower the breakeven output.

Financially, ABC has been struggling over the last 5 years, making only a very small profit in 2 of those years. Cash flow has also been an issue, with an increasing dependence upon its overdraft and the likelihood of having to extend its limit in the near future.

Being able to consolidate into one site would eventually improve ABC's position and make consistent profit a realistic possibility. In the short term, however, there is the problem of financing the purchase of the land. The situation is even more pressing due to the fact that it needs to act quickly. The best option appears to be a loan, but will the bank be willing to advance the money, especially considering the company's current cash-flow problems?

Questions

a Sketch a simple breakeven chart to illustrate how a fall in fixed costs would reduce the breakeven output. [4]
b Explain the possible benefits to ABC of using an overdraft. [6]
c Analyse the potential problems for ABC of raising the finance needed through loan capital. [9]
d To what extent do you believe achieving a positive cash flow is more important to ABC than achieving consistent profit? [16]

Answers and quick quiz 5 online

Summary

You should now have an understanding of all the points below.

Setting financial objectives

- financial objectives including those for cash flow, capital expenditure, revenue costs and profit
- the value of setting financial objectives and internal and external influences on them
- the distinction between profit and cash flow as well as between gross, operating and profit for the year

Analysing financial performance

- construction of budgets and their value including variance analysis
- construction and analysis of cash flows
- construction of, interpretation and value of breakeven charts

- illustration of changes in price, output and cost on breakeven charts
- analysis of profitability including gross, operating and profit for the year ratios
- the use of data for financial decision-making

Making financial decisions: sources of finance

- advantages and disadvantages of different sources of internal and external finance for short- and long-term purposes

Making financial decisions: improving cash flow and profits

- methods and difficulties of improving cash flow, profit and profitability

6 Decision-making to improve human resource performance

Human resources is the function of an organisation that is focused on activities related to employees. This includes manpower planning, recruitment and selection, training and development, retention and employee motivation, welfare and benefits and finally dismissal and redundancy.

Setting human resource objectives

The value of setting human resource objectives

The AQA specification outlines the following human resource objectives:
- **Employee engagement and involvement.** If employees are fully engaged and involved in the business they are more likely to be motivated, leading to higher productivity and quality of output.
- **Talent development.** This relates to the development and guidance of the future stars of a business so that they can contribute to the business success and growth. It involves not just developing their talents but also the retention of these employees.
- **Training.** The development of employee skills in order to improve performance.
- **Diversity.** This concept encompasses acceptance and respect in terms of race, gender, age sexual orientation, physical abilities, religion etc. It means understanding that each individual is unique and recognises individual differences.
- **Alignment of values.** This means bringing together employee and business values.
- **Number, skills and location of employees.** This involves manpower planning in order to ensure a business always has the right employees in the right numbers, in the right place and with the correct skills.

A business that is able to fulfil these objectives is likely to benefit from:
- a lower labour turnover
- higher labour retention rates
- higher productivity
- full compliance with any UK and EU labour legislation

Internal and external influences on human resource objectives

Human resources is no different from the other functional areas in that decision-making will be affected by a variety of external and internal factors.

External

Economy

If the economy is growing, there may be a greater requirement for human resources. Linked to this is the aspect of demographics and the availability of labour with the skills required.

Political

The UK government and the EU have passed a variety of measures that affect human resource planning, e.g. equality measures and the minimum wage.

Technology

The introduction of technology into manufacturing has resulted in not only a reduced requirement for labour but also for new skills. The decline of manufacturing and development of the service sector in terms of employment also emphasises the changing nature of work and the importance from a business perspective of developing the skills required.

Competitive environment

Changes in the market and competitor actions are likely to affect demand for a product or service, which in turn will impact on a business's human resource requirement.

Internal

Corporate objectives

Human resource objectives must be aligned with corporate objectives. If there is an overall objective of growth, human resources need to prepare for this by ensuring the availability of sufficiently skilled workers.

Type of product or service

A business must make sure the skills of the workforce are appropriate for that particular product or service as well as the image of the business.

Style of management

Whether a business has a **hard** or **soft approach** to human resource management is likely to influence decision-making. With a hard approach, managers see employees as just another resource that has to be used as efficiently as possible, whereas with a soft approach, employees are seen as a valuable asset that needs to be developed.

> A **hard human resource approach** treats employees as just another asset that must be used as efficiently as possible.
>
> A **soft human resource approach** treats employees as a valuable asset that needs to be developed.

Table 6.1 Hard and soft HR strategies

	Hard HR approach	Soft HR approach
Philosophy	Employees are no different from any other resource used by the business.	Employees are the most valuable resource available to the business and a vital competitive weapon.
Timescale	HR management operates in the short term only: employees are hired and fired as necessary.	Employees are developed over a long period of time to help the firm fulfil its corporate objectives.
Key features	• Pay is kept to a minimum. • Little or no empowerment. • Communication is mainly downwards. • Leaders have a Theory X view of the workforce. • Emphasis is on the short term in recruiting and training employees.	• Employees are empowered and encouraged to take decisions. • Leaders have a Theory Y view of the workforce. • Employees are encouraged to extend and update skills. • Employees are consulted regularly by managers. • A long-term relationship is developed with employees through use of internal recruitment and ongoing training programmes.
Associated leadership style	This approach is more likely to be adopted by leaders using an autocratic style of leadership.	This approach is more likely to be adopted by leaders using a democratic style of leadership.
Motivational techniques used	Principally financial techniques with minimal use of techniques such as delegation.	Techniques intended to give employees more control over their working lives, e.g. delegation and empowered teams.

Now test yourself

TESTED

1 Define the term 'human resource objectives' and give two examples.
2 Identify three potential benefits of having a fully engaged workforce.
3 State two internal and two external influences on human resource objectives.
4 Distinguish between a hard and a soft human resource strategy.

Answers on p. 119

Analysing human resource performance

Calculating and interpreting human resource data

REVISED

Labour turnover and retention rates

Labour turnover refers to the proportion of a business's staff leaving employment over a period of time. It is calculated as follows:

$$\frac{\text{number leaving during year}}{\text{average number of staff}} \times 100$$

> **Labour turnover** is the proportion of a business's staff leaving their employment over a period of time.

Labour retention is the number of employees with more than one year of service. It is calculated as follows:

$$\frac{\text{number of employees with one or more years of service}}{\text{overall workforce numbers}} \times 100$$

Employees may leave a business for a number of reasons:
- Low/inadequate wages levels leading employees to defect to competitors.
- Poor morale and motivation.
- A buoyant local labour market offering more attractive opportunities.

From a business point of view, lower rates of labour turnover and higher rates of labour retention are preferable, as costs of recruitment will be lower, as is the likelihood of low morale and productivity.

Labour productivity

Labour productivity is a key measure of business efficiency and measures the output per employee over a specified time period. It is calculated using the following formula:

$$\frac{\text{total output per time period}}{\text{number of employees}}$$

Higher rates of productivity are preferable, but it is important that this is not achieved at the expense of poorer quality. In addition, when comparing to other similar businesses, it is important to take into account other factors such as wage rates, technology and the way the workforce is organised.

Employee costs as a percentage of turnover

For a number of businesses, such as premiership football clubs and independent schools, labour represents their biggest cost and it is important that this is monitored and kept to a sustainable level. It is calculated as follows:

$$\frac{\text{labour costs}}{\text{turnover}} \times 100$$

Monitoring employee performance is very important to a business as it may help in identifying a business's needs in terms of recruitment, training and redundancy or redeployment.

Labour cost per unit

This measures how much it costs to produce one unit of output and is calculated as follows:

$$\frac{\text{labour costs}}{\text{output}}$$

Unit labour cost is directly related to productivity because unit labour cost will fall as each employee produces more (becomes more productive), and will rise as each worker produces less (becomes less productive).

> **Labour retention** is the proportion of employees with one or more years of service.

> **Labour productivity** measures the output per worker over a given time period.

> **Typical mistake**
>
> It is important to express answers to calculations in the correct format. When calculating productivity, for example, many students express their answers as percentages and not as a number of units of output per time period.

> **Unit labour cost** is a measure of the average labour cost of producing one unit of output.

Exam practice answers and quick quizzes at **www.hoddereducation.co.uk/myrevisionnotes**

Now test yourself

TESTED

5 Distinguish between labour turnover and labour retention.
6 A business employing 300 employees makes 25m units of output producing a £15m turnover per year. Its total labour costs are £7.5m. Calculate (i) unit labour costs and (ii) labour costs as a percentage of turnover.

Answers on p. 119

The use of data for human resource decision-making and planning

REVISED

Human resource planning is a key area of business decision making, and in order to make effective decisions, managers will require relevant information and data. Such data may be derived both internally and externally. The main aspects are summarised in Table 6.2.

Table 6.2 Summary of internal and external data

Internal	External
Productivity	Wage rates
Unit labour costs	Sales forecasts
Retention rates	Market trends
Labour turnover	Competitor actions
Skills	Unemployment rates
Age profile of workers	Skills available
Corporate objectives	Operational capacity

Once managers have analysed relevant data, key decisions can be made regarding numbers, training, skills and development of the labour force.

Exam tip

It is important to recognise that much of the data used by HR will come from other functional areas such as operations and marketing.

Now test yourself

TESTED

7 Briefly outline how a knowledge of labour turnover and market trends may affect human resource planning.

Answer on p. 119

Making human resource decisions: improving organisational design and managing the human resource flow

Influences on job design

The influences on job design are summed up in Table 6.3.

Table 6.3 Factors affecting job design

Organisational factors	Environmental factors	Behavioural factors
Task characteristics	Employee availability and ability	Feedback
Process or flow of works in organisation	Social and cultural expectations	Autonomy
Ergonomics		Variety
Work practices		

- **Organisational factors** such as the nature of the work and the culture of the business will determine the extent to which a business is able and willing to design jobs in such a way that enrichment and empowerment exist.
- **Environmental factors** that will influence job design include the availability of employees and their abilities as well as their social and cultural expectations.
- **Behavioural factors** and the extent to which a job or task/s offer autonomy, diversity and the use of skills will determine the level of enrichment and empowerment possible and impact on job design.

Job design

This is the process of deciding on the contents of a job in terms of its duties and responsibilities, on the methods used to carry out the job and on the relationships that should exist between job holder and superiors, subordinates and colleagues. Through job design or redesign, an organisation aims to make jobs interesting, challenging and rewarding with the aim of creating a fully engaged and motivated workforce. Some of the methods used include:

- **Job rotation.** This is the regular switching of employees between tasks of a similar degree of complexity. Rotating jobs provides variety and may relieve the monotony of just doing one task.
- **Job enlargement.** This extends the employees' range of duties. Instead of rotating round different tasks, the job itself is extended to include more tasks of a similar nature. This is called 'horizontal loading' and can help lessen the monotony and repetition on production lines.
- **Job enrichment.** Unlike enlargement, which is horizontally loaded, enrichment is vertically loaded with the job designed in such a way as to include more challenging tasks. Enrichment attempts to give employees greater responsibility by increasing the range and complexity of tasks they undertake with the aim of improving motivation and engagement.

Exam practice answers and quick quizzes at **www.hoddereducation.co.uk/myrevisionnotes**

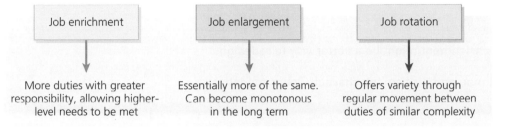

Figure 6.1 Job enrichment, enlargement and rotation

- **Empowerment.** This involves giving employees control over their working lives and can be achieved by organising employees into teams, setting them targets and allowing them to plan their own work, take their own decisions and solve their own problems.

The ideas of enrichment and empowerment have been taken further in the Hackman and Oldham job characteristics model (see Figure 6.2).

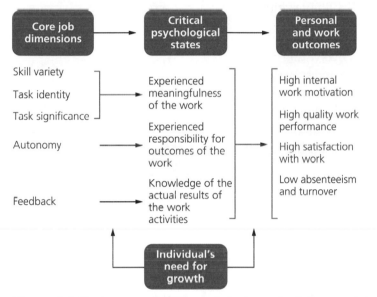

Figure 6.2 Hackman and Oldham job characteristics model

The model identifies five core characteristics (skill variety, task identity, task significance, autonomy and feedback) which impact on three critical psychological states (experienced meaningfulness, experienced responsibility for outcomes and knowledge of actual results) in turn influencing work outcomes (motivation, quality of work, job satisfaction, reduced absenteeism).

The core characteristics and psychological state operate in a continuous feedback loop, which allow employees to continue to be motivated through owning and understanding the work they are involved in. Skill variety, task identity and task significance will directly impact on the meaningfulness of the work, autonomy on responsibility and task significance on knowledge of results.

According to this model, the goal should be to design jobs in such a way that the core characteristics complement the psychological states of the worker and lead to positive outcomes. As a result, employees should achieve greater job satisfaction and motivation.

8 Briefly outline why job enrichment might be a better way to redesign a job than job rotation.
9 Briefly outline the Hackman and Oldham job characteristics model.

Answers on p. 119

Influences on organisational design

REVISED

Organisational design is the process of shaping the organisational structure so that it can achieve its objectives effectively. Key factors in organisational design are likely to be related to the span of control possible, the amount of delegation given and the level of centralisation or decentralisation. Other influences include:

- **The size of business.** The larger the business, the more complex it becomes and the greater the need for a formal organisational structure.
- **Life cycle of the organisation.** A business will evolve and change over time and, as a result, the organisational design and structure is likely to evolve with it.
- **Corporate objectives.** The organisational structure will need to fit with the corporate objectives. A business whose main objective is growth and innovation may require a different structure to one whose aim is to maintain its position in current markets.
- **Technology.** Developments in technology have changed the nature of production, impacting on organisational design and structure.

> **Organisational design** is the process of shaping an organisation's structure in order to meet its objectives effectively.

Organisational structure

An organisation is a group of people who work together to achieve a common goal. To work together effectively, a clear structure is required that defines how tasks are divided, grouped and coordinated. The structure clarifies the roles organisational members perform so that everyone understands their responsibilities to the group.

The organisational structure will often be depicted in an organisational chart. Such charts will illustrate the **hierarchy** within the business and the **chain of command** that provides a line of **authority** from the top of the business to the bottom showing who reports to whom.

The organisational chart may also show the **span of control**. This is the number of subordinates that may be controlled effectively by one manager. The span of control may depend on a number of factors such as the ability of the manager, the type of work being done and the skills of the employees. It may also be determined by whether the organisation structure is tall or flat. Organisations with wider spans of control require fewer managers and have a flatter structure, as shown in Figure 6.3a, whereas those with narrower spans are likely to have more managers and taller structures (Figure 6.3b). Flatter structures with wider spans tend to become more predominant as this gives greater scope for worker empowerment lower down the hierarchy.

> **Hierarchy** — how different levels of authority are ranked in an organisational structure.
>
> **Chain of command** is the order in which authority and power in an organisation is exercised and delegated from top management down.
>
> **Authority** is the power or right to give orders or make decisions.

> **Span of control** is the number of subordinates who can be controlled effectively by one manager.

(a)

(b)

Figure 6.3 (a) A flat hierarchy/wider span of control; (b) A tall hierarchy/narrower span of control

Flatter structures result in cost saving due to fewer middle management and can lead to greater engagement of the workforce due to more empowerment.

Influences on delegation, centralisation and decentralisation

Delegation

Delegation is the passing of authority to a subordinate within an organisation. It is the power to undertake a task that is delegated and not the responsibility for it — this remains with the manager. A manager must therefore choose delegates carefully — they must have the skills and ability to perform the task, and there has to be complete trust in the delegate. Successful delegation relieves managers of routine decisions, enabling them to concentrate on the more important decisions.

> **Delegation** is the granting of authority by one person to another for agreed purposes.

> **Typical mistake**
>
> Students often suggest responsibility can be passed down the organisation structure. This is not the case. It is authority that is passed down.

Centralisation and decentralisation

Whether an organisation is **centralised** or **decentralised** will determine where authority and decision-making lie in the organisation. A centralised structure is one where decision-making lies with management at the top with little input from lower down. A decentralised structure is one where those lower down the hierarchy play a greater part in the decision-making process.

Influences

Decentralisation will involve a greater degree of delegation, and there are a number of influences on the level of centralisation or decentralisation:

- **Uniformity of decisions.** Where decisions are uniform there is little room for delegation and decentralisation. As a result, individual outlet managers in a business such as Pizza Hut have little or no input into decision-making.
- **Management style.** An autocratic style is more likely to lead to a centralised organisation, whereas a more democratic or laissez-faire style gives greater scope for decentralisation.
- **Skills and ability of workforce.** A decentralised approach is only possible where the workforce has the necessary skills to make decisions. A business employing mainly professional skilled people is more likely to delegate and adapt a decentralised approach than one employing mainly unskilled workers.
- **Economic influences.** Changing economic circumstances can lead to different approaches. In difficult times a more centralised approach may be adopted, whereas if the economy is growing strongly there may be greater freedom for delegation and decentralisation.

> **Centralisation** is the process of concentrating management and decision-making power at the top of an organisation hierarchy.
>
> **Decentralisation** is the process of redistributing decision-making power away from a central location or authority.

- **Technology.** Developments in technology have resulted in a great deal of information being readily available to a business. This may provide greater scope for delegation and decentralisation, e.g. to individual branch or store managers.

Now test yourself

TESTED

10 Briefly outline the reasons for a business introducing a flatter organisation structure.
11 What is delegation, and why is it important to business success?
12 Distinguish between centralisation and decentralisation.
13 Identify four possible influences on organisational design.
14 Briefly explain how Tesco can operate with a certain amount of decentralisation but McDonald's cannot.

Answers on pp. 119–120

The value of changing job and organisational design

REVISED

The aim and value of changing organisational and job design is to be better able to meet human resource objectives. By making jobs more interesting, employees are likely to become more engaged and motivated, resulting in higher productivity, quality and less wastage, all of which may lead to a competitive advantage and the potential for higher revenue and profit. Changing organisational design may also lead to lower costs, particularly if it involves creating a flatter structure with fewer managerial levels.

> **Exam tip**
>
> Answers in this area frequently reveal a lack of understanding about the relationship between organisational structure and business performance. It can be a complex topic and is one you should spend time on.

Now test yourself

TESTED

15 In what ways may changing organisational and job design help in achieving human resource objectives?

Answer on p. 120

How managing the human resource flow helps meet human resource objectives

REVISED

The aim of human resources is to have the right number of people employed, with the right skills in the right place at the right time. This can be achieved creating a **human resource plan** and managing the **human resource flow**, i.e. the recruitment, selection, placement, appraisal, promotion of employees plus termination of employment.

> **Human resource planning** is the process that identifies the current and future human resource needs of an organisation in order to achieve its objectives.
>
> **Human resource flow** is the movement of employees through an organisation including recruitment, promotion and employment termination.

Recruitment and selection

The recruitment and selection process is summed up in Figure 6.4.

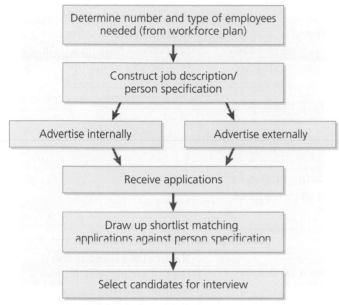

```
┌─────────────────────────────────────┐
│ Determine number and type of employees │
│        needed (from workforce plan)    │
└─────────────────────────────────────┘
                  ↓
┌─────────────────────────────────────┐
│      Construct job description/        │
│         person specification          │
└─────────────────────────────────────┘
          ↓                    ↓
┌──────────────────┐   ┌──────────────────┐
│ Advertise internally │ │ Advertise externally │
└──────────────────┘   └──────────────────┘
          ↓                    ↓
┌─────────────────────────────────────┐
│          Receive applications          │
└─────────────────────────────────────┘
                  ↓
┌─────────────────────────────────────┐
│      Draw up shortlist matching        │
│  applications against person specification │
└─────────────────────────────────────┘
                  ↓
┌─────────────────────────────────────┐
│      Select candidates for interview   │
└─────────────────────────────────────┘
```

Figure 6.4 The process of recruitment

Once the number and type of employees has been determined, **job descriptions** and **specifications** can be drawn up. The job can then be advertised both internally and externally. Internal recruitment is likely to be cheaper, but new ideas are more likely to come from external candidates. From the applications, a shortlist can be drawn up for interview, and, once interviewed and selected, the ideal candidate can be appointed.

Training

Training is the provision of job-related skills and knowledge. Almost all employees receive some training when they first start a job, known as 'induction training'. This is designed to familiarise the employee with the business procedures and policies. Training to improve the skills of the worker may be undertaken either on the job, learning from an experienced worker, or off the job at college or some other training agency.

Appraisal and promotion

Performance appraisal is the process by which a manager examines and evaluates an employee's work by comparing it to set standards, documenting the results and using these to provide feedback to employees to show where improvements need to be made. Performance appraisal can be used to determine training needs and likely candidates for promotion. Promoting from within the business is an example of internal recruitment.

Redundancy, redeployment and termination

The final stage of human resource flow is that of termination of employment or dismissal. When a job no longer exists due to the introduction of technology, moving location or closure, those employees no longer required are made redundant. The process of **redundancy**

> A **job description** sets out the duties and tasks associated with particular posts.
>
> A **job specification** sets out the qualifications and qualities required of an employee.

> **Training** is the provision of job-related skills and knowledge.

> **Performance appraisal** is a systematic and periodic process that **assesses** an employee's job performance in relation to established criteria.

> **Redundancy** is when an employee is dismissed due to their job no longer existing.

may take place on a voluntary basis, and an organisation must consult with individual employees as well as worker representatives if 20 or more employees are made redundant. Those who have been employed for over two years are entitled to redundancy pay.

As an alternative to redundancy, an employee may be offered **redeployment** within the business. This, however, may not be popular as it may involve a change of location and or changes in the conditions of work.

> **Redeployment** is the process of moving existing employees to a different job or location.

Besides redundancy, an employee may be dismissed in the following circumstances:
- **Gross misconduct**, such as violence towards a customer or colleague, or theft.
- **Persistent minor misconduct**, such as regularly turning up late for work, but only after set procedures have been adhered to in terms of verbal and written warnings.
- **A substantial reason**, such as not agreeing to new reasonable terms of employment.

It should also be noted that employment may be terminated by the employee. This might be due to family reasons or retirement. Every business expects a number of its employees to leave in this way and this is known as **natural wastage**.

> **Natural wastage** is the loss of employees from a business due to retirement, resignation or death.

Efficient management of the human resource flow providing a business with the right employees, in the right place, with the right skills should enable a business to meet its objectives more effectively.

Now test yourself

TESTED

16 Briefly explain the importance of workforce planning.

Answer on p. 120

Making human resource decisions: improving motivation and engagement

The benefits of motivated and engaged employees

REVISED

Employee engagement is a workplace approach designed to ensure that employees are committed to their organisation's goals and values and are motivated to contribute to organisational success. There are a number of potential benefits of a motivated and engaged workforce:
- **Productivity.** A fully engaged and motivated workforce is not only likely to work harder so producing more, but will probably put in the extra work to make sure deadlines are met etc.
- **Recruitment and retention.** An organisation that has a fully engaged workforce is more likely to be seen as the employer of choice, and is more likely to be able to retain its workers.
- **Absenteeism.** This is likely to be lower.

Exam practice answers and quick quizzes at **www.hoddereducation.co.uk/myrevisionnotes**

- **Innovation.** A close link has been shown to exist between innovation and engagement.
- **Profitability.** This is likely to be higher.

What is motivation?

Analysts disagree on the precise meaning of the term '**motivation**'. Some believe it is the will to work due to enjoyment of the work itself. This suggests that motivation comes from within an employee. An alternative view is that it is the will or desire to achieve a given target or goal due to some external stimulus. Many of the differences in the theories of motivation can be explained in terms of this fundamental difference of definition. Figure 6.5 shows the various schools of thought relating to motivation.

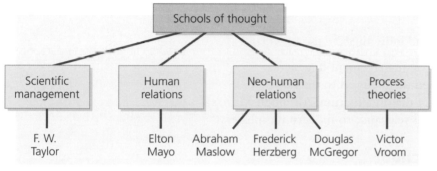

Figure 6.5 Schools of thought relating to motivation

The school of scientific management

A 'school of thought' is simply a group of people who hold broadly similar views. The school of scientific management argues that business decisions should be taken on the basis of data that are researched and tested quantitatively. Members of the school believe that it is vital to identify ways in which costs can be assessed and reduced, thus increasing efficiency. This school of thought supports the use of techniques such as work-study.

A member of the school of scientific management was **F. W. Taylor** (1856–1915). Taylor was a highly successful engineer who began to advise and lecture on management practices and was a consultant to Henry Ford. His theories were based on a simple interpretation of human behaviour.

Taylor's ideas were formulated during his time at the Bethlehem Steel Company in the USA. He believed in firm management based on scientific principles. He used a stopwatch to measure how long various activities took and sought the most efficient methods. He then detailed 'normal' times in which duties should be completed, and assessed individual performance against these. Efficiency, he argued, would improve productivity, competitiveness and profits. This required employees to be organised, closely supervised and paid according to how much they produced.

Taylor believed that people were solely motivated by money. Workers should have no control over their work, and the social aspect of employment was considered irrelevant and ignored.

Taylor's views were unpopular with shop-floor employees. As workers and managers became more highly educated, they sought other ways of motivating and organising employees.

> **Motivation** results from a range of factors that influence people to behave in certain ways.

> **Exam tip**
>
> You do not need to know any particular theory of motivation. However, you should know at least one theory of financial methods of motivation and one theory of non-financial methods of motivation.

> **Exam tip**
>
> There is not necessarily a 'right' answer as to which theory of motivation works. The success of a particular motivation technique will depend on the circumstances and the people involved.

The human relations school of management

A weakness of the scientific school was that its work ignored the social needs of employees. This, and the obvious unpopularity of the ideas, led to the development of the human relations school. This school of thought concentrated on the sociological aspects of work.

A key writer was **Elton Mayo**. He is best remembered for his Hawthorne Studies at the Western Electric Company in Chicago between 1927 and 1932. He conducted experiments to discover whether employee performance was affected by factors such as breaks and the level of lighting. The results surprised Mayo. The productivity of one group of female employees increased both when the lighting was lessened and when it was increased. It became apparent that they were responding to the level of attention they were receiving. From this experiment, Mayo concluded that motivation depends on:

- the type of job being carried out and the type of supervision given to the employee
- group relationships, group morale and individuals' sense of worth

Mayo's work took forward the debate on management in general and motivation in particular. He moved the focus on to the needs of employees, rather than just the needs of the organisation. Although Mayo's research is nearly 80 years old, it still has relevance to modern businesses.

The neo-human relations school

Abraham Maslow and **Frederick Herzberg** are recognised as key members of this school of thought. While the human relations school associated with Elton Mayo highlighted the *sociological* aspects of work, the neo-human relations school considered the *psychological* aspects of employment.

Abraham Maslow

Abraham Maslow was an American psychologist who formulated a famous hierarchy of needs (Figure 6.6). According to Maslow, human needs consist of five types that form a hierarchy:

1 **Physiological:** the need for food, shelter, water and sex.
2 **Security:** the need to be free from threats and danger.
3 **Social:** the need to love and be loved, and to be part of a group.
4 **Esteem:** the need to have self-respect and the respect of colleagues.
5 **Self-actualisation:** the need to develop personal skills and fulfil one's potential.

Maslow argued that all individuals have a hierarchy of needs and that once one level of needs is satisfied, people can be motivated by tasks that offer the opportunity to satisfy the next level of needs.

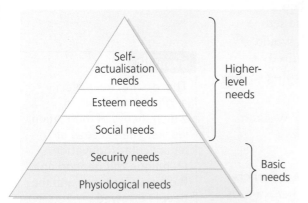

Figure 6.6 Maslow's hierarchy of needs

Some writers doubt the existence of a hierarchy of needs. They argue that social needs and esteem needs may coexist and that people do not move smoothly up a hierarchy, as Maslow's model suggests. However, his work brings psychology into motivational theory and highlights the range of individual needs that may be met through employment.

Frederick Herzberg

The research carried out by Frederick Herzberg offered some support for Maslow's views and focused on the psychological aspects of motivation. Herzberg asked 203 accountants and engineers to identify those factors about their employment that pleased and displeased them. Figure 6.7 summarises Herzberg's findings.

This research was the basis of Herzberg's two-factor theory, published in 1968. Herzberg divided the factors motivating people at work into two groups:

● **Motivators.** These are positive factors that give people job satisfaction (e.g. receiving recognition for effort) and therefore increase productivity as motivation rises.
● **Hygiene (or maintenance) factors.** These are factors that may cause dissatisfaction among employees. Herzberg argued that motivators should be built into the hygiene factors. Improving hygiene factors will not positively motivate but will reduce employee dissatisfaction. Examples of hygiene factors are pay, fair treatment and reasonable working conditions.

Herzberg did not argue that hygiene factors are unimportant. On the contrary, he contended that only when such factors are properly met can motivators begin to operate positively.

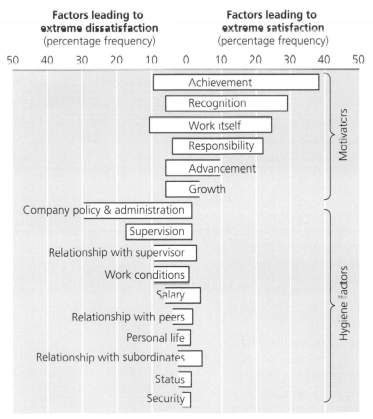

Figure 6.7 Herzberg's factors causing satisfaction and dissatisfaction

Process theories of motivation

The foremost writer on process theory is **Victor Vroom**, who published *Work and Motivation* in 1964. Vroom's theory expressed the view that motivation depends on people's expectations of the outcome. If working life offers opportunities for workers' expectations to be met, motivation is likely to be high. If the outcome of their actions is expected to be desirable, they will be motivated. The stronger the desire for the outcome, the greater is the level of motivation.

The value of theories of motivation

REVISED

The motivation theories do not set out a blueprint of how to motivate a workforce but rather their value lies in the insight they give to management and employee attitudes. Although it is easy to dismiss Taylor and the scientific school today, he did establish management as a subject worthy of study, and ideas such as time and motion study and work study are still used today by management consultants. The human relations school recognised that employees did not just work for money, and factors such as involvement in decision-making, recognition for work done well and responsibility were all important in achieving an engaged and motivated workforce. These factors are perhaps key to the non-financial methods of motivation.

Now test yourself

TESTED

17 How does the scientific school of management differ from the human relations school of management?

Answer on p. 120

How to improve employee engagement and motivation

REVISED

The benefits of a fully engaged workforce make improving engagement and motivation of the workforce an essential element of the work of the human resources function. The methods used include both financial and non-financial.

The use of financial methods of motivation

REVISED

Some writers, such as Herzberg, believe that money is not a positive motivator, although the lack of it can demotivate. Nevertheless, pay systems are designed to motivate employees financially.

Wages and salaries

Employees are normally paid a wage or salary. Wages are usually paid weekly at an hourly rate for a set working week with any extra hours (overtime) being paid at a higher rate. Salaries are expressed in annual terms but are usually paid monthly. Salaried staff do not normally have a set number of hours to work per week, although there may be a minimum number.

Piece-rate pay

Piece-rate pay gives a payment for each item produced. This system encourages effort, but often at the expense of quality. Piece rate is common in agriculture and the textile industry.

Commission

Commission is a payment made to employees based on the value of sales achieved. It can form all or part of a salary package.

Profit-related pay

Profit-related pay gives employees a share of the profits earned by the business. It encourages all employees to work hard to generate the maximum profits for the business. It also offers some flexibility: in a recession, wages can fall with profits, reducing the need for redundancies.

Performance-related pay

Performance-related pay is used in many industries, from banking to education. It needs to be tied into some assessment or appraisal of employee performance. Whatever criteria are used to decide who should receive higher pay, the effect can be divisive and damaging to employee morale.

Share ownership

Employees are sometimes offered shares in the company in which they work. Shares can be purchased through savings schemes. However, share ownership may cause discontentment if this perk is available only to the senior staff.

> **Exam tip**
>
> Do consider the financial position of the business (in terms of profits and cash flow) when developing arguments in support of and against financial methods of motivation. There is likely to be numerical evidence in a case study if such a question has been asked.

The use of non-financial methods of motivating employees

REVISED

The Hackmann Oldham job characteristics model (see p. 99) and the work of the motivation theorists give us some clues as to the non-financial methods of motivating employees. Hackmann and Oldham suggested that motivation is linked to the three psychological states: meaningful work, responsibility and knowledge of outcomes. In Herzberg's theory responsibility, involvement and recognition are key motivators, and Maslow suggested these same three factors are key in achieving self-actualisation. Key characteristics of non-financial methods of motivation can therefore be summarised as follows:

- **Meaningful work**, providing jobs that are both interesting and challenging.
- **Involvement** with the decision-making process.
- **Responsibility and recognition** for the job.

For this to be achieved it is necessary for the following to be in place:
- The **leadership and management style** is more likely to be soft and democratic.
- **Opportunity** needs to be provided for involvement and responsibility.
- The **culture** of the business needs to be one of involvement and communication.

Influences on the choice and assessment of the effectiveness of financial and non-financial reward systems

REVISED

The factors that might influence the choice and effectiveness of reward systems include:
- **Finance.** In some ways this relates to the success of an organisation as a business must operate within its means. It will also want to keep a careful check on both unit labour costs and labour costs as a percentage of turnover.
- **Nature of the work.** It is not just the type of work that will have an influence but also the skills of the workforce involved. Reward and conditions of work need to be appropriate to attract and retain employees. If a business gets this right, it may well be able to establish a reputation as a good employer to work for.
- **Culture.** The culture of the business and the management style adopted — a hard approach may favour financial incentives, whereas a soft approach may favour non-financial ones.
- **External factors.** This might include the economic cycle, e.g. it may be difficult to have performance related pay systems in times of economic recession.

Now test yourself

TESTED

18 Briefly outline the links between the non-financial methods of motivation and the motivation theories of Maslow and Herzberg.

Answer on p. 120

Making human resource decisions: improving employer–employee relations

Influences on the extent and methods of employee involvement in decision-making

REVISED

Having a fully engaged and motivated workforce requires good employer–employee relations. Employees need to feel involved and appreciated and the extent may be influenced by the following:
- **Management style.** A soft management style is more likely to lead to involvement in decision-making than a hard management style.

- **Nature of the work.** Those working in highly skilled and technical industries are more likely to have an input into decision-making than those doing unskilled repetitive tasks.
- **Legislation.** The UK government and EU legislation in terms of trade unions and works councils can have an influence on employee involvement in decision-making.

Methods of employee representation

Trade unions

A **trade union** is an organised group of employees that aims to protect and enhance the economic position of its members. They offer a number of benefits to members:

- They negotiate on pay and conditions of work.
- They discuss major changes in the work place, such as redundancy, and help protect job security.
- They provide a range of services including financial and legal advice.

When a trade union negotiates with an employer on behalf of its members on matters such as pay and conditions, it is called 'collective bargaining'. A trade union is in a much better position to negotiate than an individual worker. This not only benefits workers but also can be easier and less time-consuming for the employer.

The changing role of trade unions in the UK

Union membership has fallen steadily since its peak in 1979. This decline has been due to:

- **Legislation:** the Conservative governments of the 1980s and 1990s passed a series of measures to control the activities of trade unions.
- **Decline of traditional industries:** e.g. coal mining, steel and ship building.
- **Increasing number of small businesses:** such businesses are not strongly unionised.

There has also been a move towards union derecognition and single union agreements in workplaces.

Work councils

Workers might also be represented by **work councils**. Work councils are bodies composed of both employee and employer representatives elected to negotiate with management about working conditions, wages etc. Since they are normally elected and have both employer and employee representatives, they may provide for better communication and increased involvement of employees and result in more conciliatory relationships than those with a trade union.

> A **trade union** is an organised group of employees that aims to protect and enhance the economic position of its members.

> **Typical mistake**
>
> Trade unions are often depicted by students as being a disruptive influence in business. This approach ignores much of the good work they do in terms of conditions of work, employee protection and health and safety.

> A **work council** is a body composed of both employer and employees convened to discuss and negotiate on matters of common interest including pay and conditions.

> **Now test yourself**
>
> TESTED
>
> 19 Briefly explain why trade union membership has declined since 1979.
>
> Answer on p. 120

How to manage and improve employer–employee communications and relations

REVISED

Good relations between employer and employees do not just happen but need to be worked upon. Key to good relations is communication. If communication is effective and employees feel a part of the decision-making process, they are more likely to be engaged and motivated. This is perhaps more likely to occur where there is a soft approach to human relations.

> **Typical mistake**
>
> Many students ignore the importance of communication in fostering good relations between employers and employees. Good communication can prevent disputes and remove the need for resolution.

Advisory, Conciliation and Arbitration Service (ACAS)

Disputes, however, can and do happen and when they do, the help of ACAS can be sought. ACAS was set up by the government in 1975 as an independent body with the responsibility of preventing and resolving industrial disputes. It provides the following services:

- **Advice:** to employers, trade unions and employee associations on topics such as payment systems, absenteeism and sickness.
- **Conciliation:** it encourages continuation of negotiation rather than industrial action.
- **Arbitration:** it can act to resolve a dispute by making recommendations that may be either binding or non-binding.

ACAS can also investigate individual cases of discrimination, and overall has the aim of improving business practices to reduce the possibility of industrial disputes.

The value of good employer–employee relations

REVISED

The value of good employer–employee relations can be seen in the following areas:

- **Productivity.** Where relations are good, employees are more likely to be committed and motivated, leading to higher productivity, less wastage and better quality.
- **Employee loyalty.** Labour turnover rates are likely to be lower and retention rates higher.
- **Decision-making**. Decisions are likely to be taken faster, and the introduction of change is likely to be easier.

Now test yourself

TESTED

20 Briefly outline ACAS's main responsibility.

Answer on p. 120

Exam practice answers and quick quizzes at **www.hoddereducation.co.uk/myrevisionnotes**

Exam practice

Labour problems at XYZ plc

XYZ has been struggling to meet its human resource targets for a number of years.

	XYZ	Industry average
Labour turnover	20%	10%
Labour productivity	80	100
Unit labour costs	£10	£8

Managing director Harvey Jones has decided on a radical change of approach. He wants to move from the current hard management approach to a soft approach. This will involve flattening the present tall hierarchical structure and a significant amount of job redesign. He was partly influenced in this decision by an article he read on the Hackman Oldham job characteristics model and the importance of designing jobs with motivational properties. Further reading related to the motivational theories and particularly to Herzberg suggested that if jobs are redesigned appropriately, key motivational influences can lead to significant improvements in workforce performance.

Labour relations have not been good at XYZ and the key to the success of Harvey's plan will be in persuading the workforce to accept the ideas. For this to happen, effective communication will be necessary.

Questions

a Distinguish between a hard and soft approach to management. [4]
b Explain the possible implications for XYZ of missing its human relations targets. [6]
c Analyse the potential benefits for XYZ of job redesign. [9]
d To what extent do you believe motivational theories are useful in practice? [16]

Answers and quick quiz 6 online

ONLINE

Summary

You should now have an understanding of all the points below.

Setting human resource objectives

- the value of setting and the internal and external influences on human resource objectives

Analysing human resource performance

- the use of data in human resource planning including the calculation of labour turnover and retention, labour productivity, employee costs as a percentage of turnover and unit labour cost

Making human resource decisions: improving organisational design and managing human resource flow

- influences on job design — Hackman and Oldham model
- influences on organisational design including authority, span, hierarchy, delegation, centralisation and decentralisation

- the value of changing organisational design
- how managing human resource flow helps meet human resource objectives

Making human resource decisions: improving motivation and engagement

- the benefits of a motivated and engaged workforce and how to improve it
- the value of theories of motivation — Taylor, Maslow and Herzberg
- financial and non-financial methods of motivation and influences on their choice and effectiveness

Making human resource decisions: improving employer–employee relations

- the value of good employer–employee relations
- influences on and methods of employee involvement including trade unions and works councils
- how to manage and improve employer–employee relations

Now test yourself answers

1 What is business?

1 Three reasons business exist include:

  (i) to provide goods and services

  (ii) to develop a good idea (enterprise)

  (iii) to provide help and support to others

2 A mission statement paints the broad picture. The objectives of a business are more specific — they are targets or goals that will enable a business to achieve its overall mission.

3 Five business objectives are:

  (i) growth

  (ii) survival

  (iii) profit

  (iv) customer service

  (v) corporate social responsibility

4

Type of organisation	Objectives
Public limited company	Profit, growth
Public sector organisation	Service, social and economic benefits for community
Charity	Fundraising and support for charity

5 The mission statement sets out the vision of the business and its core purpose and focus. Overall corporate and strategic planning can then be set and measured against the core purpose.

6 SMART means specific, measurable, achievable, realistic and time based. By having SMART objectives it is possible to evaluate the success in achieving them.

7 profit = total revenue – total costs

  £50,000 – £5,000 – £30,000

  profit = £15,000

8 (i) Corporate businesses have limited liability, unlike non-corporate businesses.

  (ii) Corporate businesses can sell shares and have shareholders.

  (iii) Corporate businesses (especially plcs) are generally much larger.

9 The public sector is that part of the economy owned and controlled by the government or local authorities, e.g. NHS, fire service and rubbish collection.

10 (i) To help the local community, possibly by providing essential services.

  (ii) To help people to acquire job-related skills to assist them into employment.

  (iii) To buy products from overseas under fair-trading schemes offering benefits to producers in less developed countries.

11 Mutuals are owned collectively by a business's clients or members, whereas incorporated businesses are owned by its shareholders.

12 Most new businesses are set up as sole traders because they are usually small, mostly local businesses, and a sole trader is the simplest and easiest business to form.

13 (i) Changing circumstances such as growth of the business.

  (ii) Capital — it may be easier to raise capital as a plc.

  (iii) Takeover may cause a change of legal structure.

14 (i) To earn income resulting from a share of the profit of the business in the form of a dividend.

  (ii) For capital growth — if the business does well, the share price is likely to increase, resulting in an increase in the value of an investment.

15 (i) increased profit

  (ii) expectancy of increased profit

  (iii) changes in the market

  (iv) world uncertainty

16 market capitalisation = share price × number of shares issued

  = 57p × 2,100m

  = £1,197m

17 If sales are to be achieved in a competitive market, a business must make its product or service stand out from the rest. It must make it different, i.e. differentiate it from the rest. If it can do this successfully it is likely to gain a competitive advantage and therefore increased sales and potentially profit.

18 A rise in interest rates is likely to result in lower disposable income for consumers. This is due to the fact that many will be making higher interest payments on loans and overdrafts, whilst others may be inclined to save more. If spending is reduced, manufacturers of luxury products are likely to be the ones that suffer most.

19 A study of demographics is important as:

  (i) Population affects the level of demand.

  (ii) The make-up of the population, age, income, occupation etc. affects the nature of goods bought.

  (iii) An understanding of the structure of the working population will have implications for employment.

20 Fair trade is a movement that strives for fair treatment of farmers in less developed countries.

2 Managers, leadership and decision-making

1 Four key aspects of a leader's role are:

  (i) setting objectives

  (ii) organising the way work is performed

  (iii) motivating and communicating

  (iv) analysing and appraising performance

2 Three influences on leadership style are:

  (i) the leader's personality and skills

  (ii) the nature of the industry

  (iii) the culture of the business

3 A democratic leader makes the final decision but involves others in the process.

  A laissez-faire leader allows team members freedom in doing their work and meeting deadlines.

4 In the Tannenbaum Schmidt continuum leaders are classified according to how much they tell or listen to workers.

5 A decision tree requires the following three key pieces of information:

  (i) the cost of each decision

  (ii) the financial outcome

  (iii) the probability

6 Decision trees have the benefit that they make managers think about and quantify outcomes, which can help reduce risk in decision-making. They do, however, have the drawback that they can be open to a manager's bias — outcomes and probabilities may be made more favourable in order to have a particular decision accepted.

7 The external environment may have a big impact on decision-making. A downturn in the economy or rise in interest rates could see decisions being postponed or even abandoned altogether, whereas an expanding economy or fall in interest rates might see decisions being brought forward.

8 (i) competition

  (ii) resources available

  (iii) ethics

  (iv) business objectives

9

Stakeholder	Interest
Employees	job security, good working conditions and pay
Customers	good customer service and value for money
Shareholders	capital growth and dividends
Suppliers	regular orders and on-time payment

10 Mendelow categorises stakeholders according to the amount of power they have and their level of interest.

11 (i) leadership style

  (ii) state of the economy

  (iii) business objectives

  (iv) government

12 The key to managing stakeholder relations is likely to be good communication with participation and involvement in decision-making.

3 Decision-making to improve marketing performance

1 Sales volume refers to the number of units sold. Sales value represents the value in monetary terms of those sales.

2 If the actual market is increasing in size faster than an individual company's market share, then sales will rise but market share fall.

3 If a business can achieve brand loyalty, not only will it mean returning customers and maintaining market share, but these customers are also likely to recommend the product to others.

4 **Internal:** (i) finance available, (ii) production capacity, (iii) human resources

  External: (i) economy, (ii) competition, (iii) ethics

5 total market size = (sales/market share) × 100

  30/5 = £6m × 100 = £600m total market size

6 Primary market research differs from secondary in that it is:

  (i) first-hand information

  (ii) specific to the purpose required

  (iii) more expensive to collect

7 Qualitative market research is designed to discover the attitudes and opinions of consumers that influence their purchasing behaviour. A food manufacturer might use a consumer panel to test a new chocolate bar and receive detailed opinions on the taste and texture of the new product.

  Quantitative market research is the collection of information on consumer views and behaviour that can be analysed statistically. This type of research might be used to investigate whether a new product is likely to achieve a sufficient volume of sales to make it financially viable.

8 A business is unlikely to have either the time or the financial resources to interview the whole of the population so it will therefore interview only a small relevant sample when undertaking market research. This saves the business both time and money.

9 Correlation is a statistical technique used to establish the extent of a relationship between two variables such as sales and adverting.

Extrapolation analyses the past performance of sales and uses this to forecast the future trend of sales.

10 The confidence interval in market research is the margin of error. In this case, if 60% of all respondents (sample) prefer a particular soap, market research analysts can be confident that between 55 and 65% of the overall population would prefer that brand.

11 A figure of −2.3 indicates elastic demand (ignore the minus sign). As a result, a price increase would result in a fall in demand and therefore a decline in revenue.

12 Spending on luxury items requires consumers to have disposable income. This means spending on luxuries will be greater when income is rising and less when it is falling as in the recession of 2008. This means spending on luxuries is responsive to changes in income, i.e. it is income elastic.

13 Market targeting results in more effective marketing as it can be directed specifically at the target group and convey a clear message relative to the positioning of the product or service. Resources will also be used more effectively as a result of the targeted marketing approach.

Market targeting may, however, result in potentially profitable segments being overlooked. It may also be the case that changes in taste and fashion could be missed.

14 Mass market refers to the whole market, whereas a niche is a small part of that larger market, e.g. Ford aims its cars at the whole market, whereas Porsche targets a small section of the car market.

15 People, process and physical environment have been included in the marketing mix of 4Ps due to the growth of the service sector and the importance of these Ps to that sector.

16 A marketing manager is likely to take into consideration market research and the nature of the product when designing a marketing mix. Market research may reveal information regarding an acceptable price for consumers or details about particular functions of the product. The nature of the product is also likely to be used to determine where it is sold and the price charged.

17 The Boston matrix allows businesses to undertake product portfolio analysis based on the product's market growth rate and its market share. It classifies products into four categories and helps managers to have products in each one.

The product life cycle is the theory that all products follow a similar pattern, moving through five stages during their life. Its use can avoid circumstances where firms have a range of products all in declining popularity.

18 A cash cow is a product that has a large share of a market that is growing quickly. A problem child is a product that has a small share of a market that is growing quickly.

19 Pricing strategies are the medium- to long-term pricing plans that a business adopts. Pricing tactics are a series of pricing techniques that are normally used only over the short term to achieve specific goals such as increasing sales.

20 Price skimming may be appropriate when a new product is launched onto the market, especially if it has unique selling points that differentiate it from rivals' products.

21 The promotional mix includes advertising, public relations, direct selling and merchandising.

22 Two influences on the promotional mix are the amount of finance available and the target market. Finance is likely to be limited for a new business and will need to be carefully budgeted. The restaurant's target market will also have an impact — is it targeting low- or high-income diners? The promotional mix will be determined accordingly.

23 Tesco sells its products both in its shops and on line. It also operates a click and collect service.

24 The people selling a product and the process used can make or break the sale of that product, so they are just as important as they are for selling a service.

25 Product life cycle and positioning will affect the marketing mix in that a product in the growth stage of the product life cycle will require a different mix to one in the maturity stage. In addition, in terms of positioning, a convenience product will require a different mix to a luxury product.

26 Digital marketing has benefited businesses in that they have the ability to gather more detailed information about consumers and to build relationships with them. For example, through its loyalty card Tesco can target promotions at individual customers.

4 Decision-making to improve operational performance

1 Added value is an amount added to the value of a product or service, equal to the difference between its cost and the amount received when it is sold.

2 Operations needs to liaise with marketing as it will make forecasts from market research as to what and how much should be produced. It will also be necessary to liaise with finance as this function will determine budgets and the availability of finance for capital investment, e.g. into technology.

3 Capacity refers to the maximum (total) amount a business can produce in a set time period.

Capacity utilisation is a measure of the proportion of total capacity that is being used in that time period.

4 capacity utilisation = output/maximum output × 100

20,000/25,000 × 100 = 80%

labour productivity = output/number of employees

20,000/75 = 266.66 units per employee

unit costs of production = total costs of production/ number of employees

£1m/25,000 = £40

5 Unit costs of production will decline when capacity utilisation and productivity increase in the short term only — variable costs will increase and the fixed costs will be spread across more units of output.

6 Two advantages of JIT production are lower costs due to the reduced need for storage space and lower wastage as there is less likelihood of products being damaged or going out of fashion.

Two disadvantages are production may be halted if stock fails to arrive on time due to weather or other problems. Costs may also be higher due to missing out on bulk purchase discounts.

7

Benefits	Drawbacks
If achieved by introduction of technology, quality and reliability may improve.	Resistance of employees.
Job redesign and training may improve motivation.	Cost.
	Quality may fall, e.g. if piece rate is used.

8 A capital-intensive approach to production puts a greater emphasis on capital than labour in production. This will benefit a UK manufacturing business as labour is expensive in the UK so such an approach will help reduce overall costs of production and increase competitiveness.

9 Excess production capacity occurs when a business is producing below maximum capacity.

A lack of production capacity occurs when demand is greater than the maximum capacity level.

10 Capacity utilisation may be improved by increasing sales or reducing the maximum capacity. Increasing sales might be achieved through better marketing or targeting new markets. Reducing capacity involves selling off unwanted production capacity but this should only be done if a business is sure that the capacity is no longer needed.

11 Some examples of the implications of a decision to use new technology:

(i) Marketing	(ii) Finance
New production processes allowing lower prices or new products increasing sales.	Initial costs but possibly resulting in increased profits in the long term.
(iii) Operations management	**(iv) People in business**
The use of technology may assist a business in meeting its quality targets.	Production line technology may increase productivity.

12 Quality is important as it may provide a USP for a business. This could enhance its reputation with consumers and lead to word-of-mouth promotion.

13 Total quality management instils a culture of quality throughout the business. Quality issues should be spotted at an early stage as everyone is responsible, thereby reducing costs and wastage.

14 Poor quality is likely to lead to increased costs as a result of wastage and the cost of replacing or repairing returned goods.

15 If the nature of product is perishable, less inventory will be held. If demand is seasonal, the level of inventory is likely to be higher than for products that have regular demand.

16 Four key features of an inventory control chart are:

(i) maximum inventory level

(ii) reorder level

(iii) buffer inventory level

(iv) lead time

17 Payment terms may be more important when a business has concerns over cash flow and a longer payment period may be beneficial.

18 Mass customisation is the tailoring of goods to specific customer requirements. In other words, customers build their own products. This is likely to give a business a competitive advantage and greater customer satisfaction. For example, in the car industry customers can build their own vehicle in terms of colour, trim and accessories.

19 Demand is likely to be higher during school holidays, therefore prices can be higher during these periods and lower at other times. In addition, at the start and end of the season when snow is less reliable, prices are likely to be lower and there may be more promotions.

20

Advantages of outsourcing	Disadvantages of outsourcing
Respond quicker to increases in demand.	Likely to be more expensive.
Dependability for consumers.	Quality may not be as good.
Lower costs as do not have to invest in capacity.	

5 Decision-making to improve financial performance

1 A profitable business may fail due to cash-flow problems. Although sales may have been generated to make a profit, not all money from these sales may have been received, causing cash-flow problems and in the worst case failure.

2 **Gross profit** is the difference between sales revenue and the direct costs of production.

   Operating profit is the difference between gross profit and the indirect costs of production (expenses).

   Profit for the year takes into consideration other expenditure such as tax and interest payments, and other income, such as interest, to arrive at a final profit figure.

3 return on investment = return from investment (or profit)/capital invested × 100

4 A rise in interest rates is likely to both increase costs and reduce demand. Costs will rise due to higher interest payments on loans, and demand fall due to lower disposable income of consumers.

5 A business might not be able to achieve financial targets in favourable market conditions due to a lack of resources, e.g. production capacity or skilled labour.

6

Favourable variances	Response
Higher sales than expected.	Increase production.
Lower fixed costs.	Possibly reduce prices.
Reduced fuel costs.	Enjoy increased profits.
Reduced material costs.	Lower prices or enjoy higher profits.

Adverse variances	Response
Sales below forecast.	Increase advertising.
Wage costs higher than forecast.	Use more technology in production.
Material costs higher than forecast.	Seek new suppliers.
Profits below forecast.	Seek new markets.

7 Three benefits of budgeting are:

   (i) Budgets mean that targets can be set and monitored for each part of the business.

   (ii) Budgets may improve financial control by preventing overspending.

   (iii) They bring focus to decision-making as a result of individual managers having to think about the financial implications of decisions.

8 breakeven = fixed costs/contribution per unit

9 contribution = sales revenue − variable costs

   sales revenue = £100,000 × 2.50 = £250,000

   variable costs = £100,000 × 1.50 = £150,000

   contribution total = £250,000 − £150,000 = £100,000

10 (i) breakeven = fixed costs/contribution per unit

   fixed costs = £15,000

   contribution per unit = 5 − 3 = 2

   breakeven output = 15,000/2 = 7,500 units

   (ii) profit = total revenue − total costs

   total revenue = £10,000 × 5 = £50,000

   total costs = £15,000 + £10,000 × 3 = £45,000

   profit = £50,000 − £45,000 = £5,000

11 A rise in fixed costs will cause the breakeven output to increase.

   An increase in price will lead to a fall in the breakeven output.

12 Breakeven analysis assumes that all output is sold and that it is all sold at the same price, neither of which are likely in practice.

13 Gross profit margin might be improving as a result of falling direct costs of production but, if the indirect costs are increasing at a higher rate, the operating profit margin could be falling.

14 Payables: money owed for goods and services that have been purchased on credit.

Receivables: money owed by a business's customers for goods or services purchased on credit.

15 A cash-flow forecast is important because:

(i) It can be used in support of loan applications.

(ii) It may identify periods when a business might be short of cash so corrective action can be taken.

(iii) It may help in the planning for items of capital expenditure.

16 An overdraft is flexible as the business only pays interest on the amount that it borrows, but it is repayable on demand.

A bank loan is normally for a fixed amount and repayable over a period of time.

17 Retained profit and equity may be preferable sources of finance due to the fact they do not have to be paid back and there are no interest charges.

18

Cause	Solution
Poor management	Training or recruiting skilled managers.
Giving too much trade credit	Offer shorter periods or negotiate more favourable terms from suppliers.
Overtrading	Plan the financial aspects of growth thoroughly.
Unexpected expenditure	Have a contingency fund to meet such demands.

19 Two ways of increasing profit are:

(i) increasing prices

(ii) reducing costs

20 Increasing prices could lead to a fall in demand and revenue unless the product is price inelastic.

Costs might be reduced at the expense of quality, which might damage reputation.

6 Decision-making to improve human resource performance

1 Human resource objectives are the targets set specifically by and for the human resources function and might include targets for labour productivity and labour turnover.

2 Potential benefits of a fully engaged workforce are:

(i) higher productivity

(ii) lower labour turnover

(iii) greater labour retention

3 Two internal influences on human resource objectives: style of management used and the type of product produced.

Two external factors: the economy and technology.

4 A hard human resource approach treats employees as just another asset that must be used as efficiently as possible.

A soft human resource approach treats employees as a valuable asset that needs to be developed.

5 Labour turnover is a measure of the proportion of a business's staff leaving their employment during the course of a year.

Labour retention is the proportion of employees with one or more years of service in the business.

6 (i) unit labour costs = labour costs/number of employees = £7.5m/300 = £25,000

(ii) labour costs as a percentage of turnover = labour costs/turnover × 100

$7.5m/15m × 100 = 50\%$

7 A knowledge of labour turnover and market trends will help in human resource planning as it will help identify needs in terms of recruitment, training, and redundancy or redeployment.

8 Job rotation simply allows employees to move around the factory floor undertaking different jobs at the same level. Job enrichment, however, provides more challenging tasks which are likely to be more motivating for employees.

9 The Hackman and Oldham model identifies five core characteristics (skill variety, task identity, task significance, autonomy and feedback), which impact on three critical psychological states (experienced meaningfulness, experienced responsibility for outcomes and knowledge of actual results) in turn influencing work outcomes (motivation, performance, job satisfaction and absenteeism).

10 A flatter organisation structure may be introduced in order to reduce costs and to give greater responsibility to employees in their work environment.

11 Delegation is the granting of authority by one person to another for agreed purposes. It is important in that it allows managers to concentrate on the more important strategic decision-making and it gives subordinates valuable experience.

12 Centralisation is the concentration of management and decision-making power at the top of an organisation hierarchy.

Decentralisation is the process of redistributing decision-making power away from a central location or authority.

13 Four possible influences on organisational design are:

(i) size of the business

(ii) life cycle of the organisation

(iii) corporate objectives

(iv) technology

14 McDonald's relies on the uniformity of its product and service which customers trust and enjoy and it cannot afford to allow individual managers to change that. Tesco, however, can allow individual store managers to respond to both the nature of demand and changes to demand in different parts of the country.

15 Changing organisational and job design is likely to make jobs more interesting and challenging which in turn may improve employee motivation. As a result, workers may become more engaged thus increasing productivity, lowering labour turnover and increasing labour retention.

16 Effective workforce planning enables a business to have the right employees in the right place and with the right skills, making it more likely a business will achieve both its human resources and corporate objectives.

17 The scientific school of management is concerned with the needs of the organisation and the way the job is done rather than the needs of the individual, simply believing employees are motivated by money. The human relations school recognises that the needs of the individual employee are also important in improving motivation and efficiency.

18 The non-financial methods of motivation revolve around making work more challenging and interesting, achieved by giving greater responsibility and involvement in the decision-making process. Responsibility and involvement are key motivators in Herzberg's theory and are essential in achieving self-actualisation in Maslow's theory.

19 Trade union membership has declined since 1979 due to the changing nature of employment. Traditional industries. such as coal and steel, have declined and employment has fallen in manufacturing — both these areas tended to be highly unionised. The service industry has seen a growth of employment but is less unionised. In addition, there has been a growth in self-employment and small businesses, which are less unionised.

20 ACAS's main responsibility is to prevent or resolve industrial disputes.